NATIVE AMERICAN
ART AND FOLKLORE

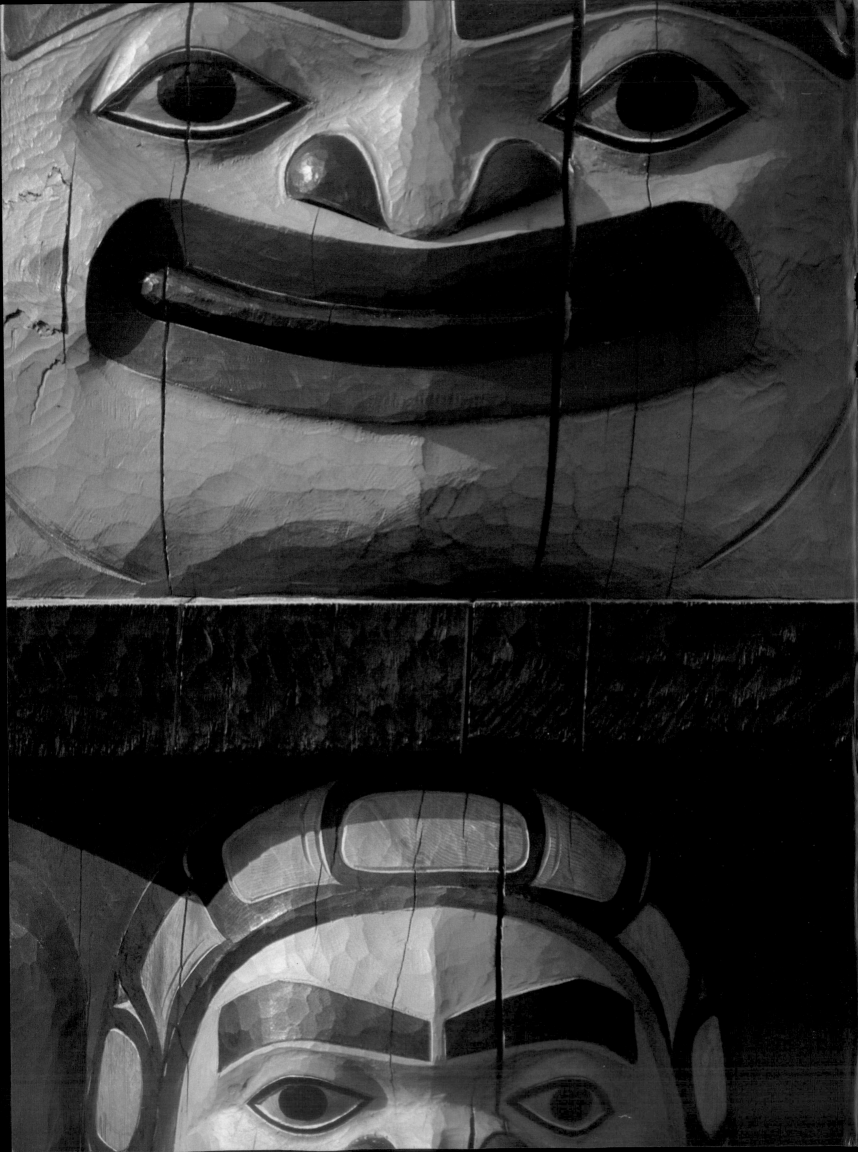

NATIVE AMERICAN
ART AND FOLKLORE

A CULTURAL CELEBRATION

EDITED BY
DAVID CAMPBELL

This 1993 edition published by Crescent Books,
distributed by Outlet Book Company, Inc.,
a Random House Company,
40 Engelhard Avenue,
Avenel, NJ 07001.

Produced by
Brompton Books Corporation
15 Sherwood Place,
Greenwich, CT 06830

ISBN 0-517-06975-X

8 7 6 5 4 3 2 1

Printed and bound in Hong Kong

Designer and Picture Editor: Bill Yenne

Picture Credits

Tony Abeyta 105, 106, 107
Mary Adair 39 (left)
AGS Archives 122-123
Alaska Division of Tourism 200
Courtesy of Bellas Artes Gallery, Santa Fe, NM 196
Jon Blumb 35, 36, 37, 90, 140, 141
SS Burrus 34 (both)
Collection of Bill Yenne 13, 62-63
Courtesy of Copeland Rutherford Fine Arts Ltd, Santa Fe, NM 46, 47
© Tom Debolski 64 (both), 65
David D DuBois 142 (both), 143
© Richard L Faller 147
Courtesy of Gallery 10, Inc, Scottsdale, AZ and Santa Fe, NM 92, 93, 94, 95, 98, 99, 100, 101, 102, 103
Craig Dan Goseyun 91
Joan Hill 42, 43, 44, 45
Institute of American Indian Arts Museum, Permanent Collection, Santa Fe, NM, Photographer Larry Phillips 109, 153, 197
© Jerry Jacka 144, 145
Anthony Jojola 104 (both)
© Joyner Publications, Ltd 152
© Lisa Law 108
Courtesy of LewAllen Gallery, Santa Fe, NM 96, 97, 110, 111, 148, 149, 150, 151
Lowie Museum of Anthropology, University of California at Berkeley 26 (left), 27, 29, 30, 31, 76, 81, 83, 87, 89, 130, 154, 155, 156, 158 (bottom), 178, 179, 180, 182 (left), 185, 192, 193, 203, 204 (both), 205, 208, 210 (left), 211, 212 (both), 213
Joan McCarthy 80
© MarLyn 146 (right)
Courtesy of Moondance Gallery, Santa Fe, NM 138, 139
National Archives 12 (left), 14, 48, 49, 51, 52, 113, 114 (top), 117, 131, 198
Nevada State Museum 172
New Mexico State Economic Development/Tourist Board 60
Gary Robinson 10, 11
Shalah Rowlen 32 (right), 33
San Francisco State University 24, 25, 26 (right), 78, 79, 82 (all), 84 (all), 85, 86 (all), 88 (all), 132, 134, 135, 136, 158 (top left and right), 159 (top), 161 (all), 165 (right), 166 (both), 167, 168 (both), 169, 173, 174, 176, 177, 182 (right), 183, 184 (all), 190, 202, 206, 207, 209, 210 (right), 214, 215, 216, 217
Connie Seabourn 40 (both), 41
Smithsonian Institution, National Anthropological Archives 8-9, 12 (right), 15 (both), 114 (bottom), 115, 116, 117, 157, 164-165
Smithsonian Institution, National Collection of Fine Arts 112, 133
Smithsonian Institution, National Museum of Natural History 25, 77, 137, 175, 191
South Dakota Tourism 128 (both)
Dorothy Strait 32 (left)
Nowetah Timmerman 38 (left top and bottom)
Kevin Skypainter Turner 39 (right)
United States Department of the Interior, Bureau of Land Management, Anasazi Heritage Center 66, 67, 68, 69, 70, 71, 72 73, 74, 75
University of Kentucky 28, 181
Charles Go Vann 38 (right)
Denise Wallace 218 (both), 219, 220, 221
© Carolyn Wright 146 (left)
© Bill Yenne 2, 58-59, 63, 157 (top left, center and right), 159 (bottom), 160, 186 (both), 187, 188 (both), 189, 194, 195, 224

Page 1: This Haida motif from British Columbia's Queen Charlotte Islands includes a stylized illustration of a whale. The small circle *(top right)* that looks like an ear, actually represents the whale's blowhole.

Page 2: These almost whimsical representations smile from a Tlingit totem pole on display in Juneau, Alaska. The pole was completed in the twentieth century, but the style and palate are quite traditional.

Overleaf: The Taos Pueblo in New Mexico is one of the largest of these ancient cities still extant. Although the Taos Pueblo is open to the public, it is still maintained largely in its original condition.

TABLE OF CONTENTS

PREFACE

his book serves as a celebration of Native American culture. It is designed as a straightforward representation of the art and folklore of North America's native peoples, containing both ceremonial and decorative works, dating from prehistory to the 1990s, as well as some of the traditional legends of the peoples from the four corners of North America. The geographical breakdown represented here indicates the regions of North America as they are generally recognized by ethnographers.

All Native North American peoples possess religious beliefs and practices that shaped their daily lives, and thus, their art and folklore, which are strongly influenced by this, to an extent similar to European cultures. All tribes traditionally shared a belief in the life of the spirit after death and a pantheon of gods and spiritual personalities with the ability to intervene in the affairs of humans. They came to believe that all natural things, animal and otherwise, possessed supernatural power and magic. From the earliest days of their cultural evolution, most Native American communities had medicine men, shamans or

These pages: Haida totem poles at Old Kasaan Village in southeastern Alaska. Poles in the foreground show the crests of Chief Skowl, who died in 1882. The literal translation of this crest is: 'Raven stealing the Sun; raven putting back his beak after having lost it on the hook of the halibut fisherman; grizzly bear and the young woman or the cubs.'

These Pages: Woodrow Haney, a Muscogee Creek chief, instructs a youngster in tribal culture, demonstrating on a wooden flute. Haney was photographed in 1983 by Gary Robinson, a Muscogee Creek Nation communication specialist.

priests, who were people in especially close contact with the supernatural and who interceded on behalf of others.

Native Americans of all cultures shared certain ceremonial occasions. Out of a deep respect for their natural environment and because they knew that all supplies are ultimately limited, these people prayed for replenishment; appeasing the gods was always done before harvest and hunts. They also had important ceremonies associated with both birth and death.

Naturally, such cultures so rich in mythology, ritual and spirituality spawn art which reflects these aspects. However, Native American art not only reflects the myths, it incorporates it in the form of ceremonial masks representing supernatural personalities, idols of revered gods, tools of magic and other creations full of symbology of the culture. Native American art not only mirrors these cultures, it is an integral component of them.

Art is so much a part of Native American cultures because a great deal of it is functional: decorated utilitarian objects, cooking vessels, tools, weapons and costumes. Designs used on ritual objects and costumes were thought to produce the magic or religious quality that distinguished these sacred objects from secular ones.

Some cultures also had a full-time artist who produced art objects for wealthy patrons, shamans and chiefs, which were admired as fine examples of technique and form, independent of function. After contact with Europeans, however, some artistic expression slanted toward trade with whites, leading to the creation of many objects which had little function in native cultures.

It is appropriate in this preface to cite the work of the late nineteenth century ethnologist Francis La Flesche (1857-1932), who did much to keep alive our knowledge of the subtle nuances of Native American culture. In 1881, La Flesche began his work with the office of the US Commissioner of Indian Affairs, and in 1910, he transferred to the Smithsonian Institution's Bureau of American Ethnology. By the time he retired on 26 December 1929, he had written numerous articles for scholarly publications and had become widely published in ethnographic circles.

Writing in 1900, La Flesche observed that white people in the United States of the late nineteenth century spoke of the area west of the Mississippi as a 'wilderness,' as though it were an empty track without human interest or history. 'To us Indians, it was as clearly defined then as it is today,' said La Flesche. 'We knew the boundaries of tribal lands, those of our friends and those of our foes; we were familiar with every stream, the contour of every hill, and each peculiar feature of the landscape had its tradition. It was our home, the scene of our history, and we loved it as our country.'

La Flesche's words clearly articulate the white European culture's most widely held misconception of Native American culture, a misconception that is slowly being overturned in the latter years of the twentieth century.

La Flesche noted that Native American tribal rites, which for generations running back beyond the historic period, were to the native people their law and their religion.

Even in the early twentieth century, he noted, these traditions were rapidly dying, as were the few old men to whom these rites had been transmitted with reverent care. La Flesche saw that, under the conditions and because of the ideas introduced among the people by the whites, these rites would soon fade from the memory of future generations and be lost beyond recovery. It was because of these changes that La Flesche gave his ardent attention to the ceremonial life of the people.

Above: Tsacotna and Natsanitna, two Tlingit girls from Cooper River in Alaska, show off their decorated clothing and jewelry in this 1903 photograph. Tlingits were avid traders and bargained for brass buttons that they turned into nose rings. In later years, mother of pearl buttons became available and were applied to clothing and blankets as trimming. Buttons and dentalium jewelry were symbols of status among Northwest tribes. In the past, when young girls like these reached a marriageable age, they wore a labret or plug in the lower lip and the family tattoo on the outside of their hand.

Above Right: Two young Comanche girls are wearing decorated buckskin dresses in this 1891-93 photograph taken on the Kiowa Reservation in Oklahoma. On the left is Wanada Parker, daughter of Quanah Parker, the first recognized chief of all Comanche.

Most memorable was La Flesche's study of the Osage tribe and the rite called Ga-hí-ge O-kón, or the Rite of the Chiefs. Shamans also handed down stories of the tribe's experiences, but in cryptic form, the clear meanings of which were revealed only to the studious members of the tribe. These men were well aware of the historic facts of the tribal life of the people, as well as their tribal institutions, and that rites and traditions developed gradually.

La Flesche saw this gradual development as a process continually stimulated not only by a tribe's desire for the preservation of tribal existence, but by actual hard experiences which taxed both the physical and mental powers of the people and their leaders. Rites also recalled a time when the life of the people as a tribe was in a chaotic state, and chronicled their emergence therefrom to their achievement of a tribal government well suited to safeguard the people, as an organized body, from internal and external perils.

Among the Osage, as among other tribes, there were rituals and traditions about what La Flesche termed the 'Sayings of Ancient Men.' In these, the tribe recorded the thoughts that occupied the minds of the shamans and storytellers when they were formulating principles, which were regarded by ancient men as fundamental to the tribal organization. These principles guided the people in tribal existence.

Every rite to which native people clung from the earliest times of their tribal existence was regarded by them as religious and supplicatory in character.

Those relating to war, to peace and to life were held with equal veneration. The thoughts embodied in the symbolic tribal organization and in the formulated rites were gathered by the shamans from the open book of nature, not in a single season, nor even in a single lifetime, but through years of patient mental toil.

The native people also learned that as a tribe they must daily appeal to natural forces for a long, healthful life. Therefore, at dawn, when they saw the reddened sky signaling the approach of the Sun, men, women and children stood in the doors of their houses and uttered their prayer for divine help. As the Sun reached midheaven, they repeated their prayer, and their supplications again arose as the Sun touched the western horizon.

The thoughts of ancient shamans, the continual theme of which was life, were given expression not only in formulated rites, but also in symbols and artwork, which were often more expressive than words. The tribal organization, for instance, symbolically expresses the idea conceived by men who saw that the part of the universe visible to them was a great unit, and that life issues from the combined force and influence of the various bodies that compose the unit.

This expression was emphasized in the recited parts of many rituals of the tribal rites, which told of the descent of the people from the sky to take possession of the Earth and make it their abode. In their rituals, the Native Americans often went so far as to personify the various aspects of the natural world, as did the Egyptians, Hindus and the people of the Greco-Roman culture.

As La Flesche noted, the ancient shamans and artists had arrived at the conception that 'all life issues, which take on manifold forms, result from the combined influence of two great physical forces–namely, the Sky, including all the heavenly bodies, and the Earth, including the waters distributed over it, and represented this duality in tribal organization. The duality was also reflected in all tribal rites, those which pertained to war and those which related to peace and civil government.'

Art was also a very important part of the ceremonial life of Native Americans, as La Flesche cited in his description of the Kí-non, the ceremonial painting of the Xó-ka (Initiator). 'At dawn of the day appointed for the initiation, the candidate went with his Shó-ka to the house of the Xó-ka. Xó-ka was the title of a man who acted as initiator in the initiatory ceremonies of a tribal rite. Such a man had to be one who had taken the degree he conferred. He could choose his own candidate or be chosen by a man offering himself as a candidate for initiation into the degree.

'The Shó-ka carries with him the skin of a black bear, the skin of a swan and a woven belt, all of which articles are to be worn by the Xó-ka as his sacerdotal apparel. The Shó-ka also takes with him a wooden bowl, in which is put pulverized charcoal mixed with water, the ceremonial paint to be used by the Xó-ka. When the candidate and his Shó-ka have entered and are assigned to their places in the lodge, the Xó-ka strips himself of his own clothing, preparatory to putting on his official apparel. When about to paint himself with the charcoal, the Xó-ka recites a wí-gi-e, called Xó-ka Wí-gi-e, which is in three parts. The first relates to the Black Bear and to certain symbols given by that animal to the people.'

The same use of imagery La Flesche describes was true throughout most of the native people of America, from the Northwest coast, where the animals of the Haida totem pole represented forces of nature identified with specific clans, to the Southwest, where Hopi kachinas portrayed aspects of human interaction with nature.

Our objective in this volume is to let the art and literature speak for itself without extensive commentary, but we should point out that throughout, one is constantly reminded of the unique bond that North America's native people had with the Earth itself and the forces of the natural world upon it.

–David Campbell and Rebecca Gulick, 1992

Above: Francis La Flesche, the noted Omaha ethnologist, at the time of his being awarded an honorary doctorate from the University of Nebraska. Because of his scholarly contributions to the study of the Omaha Indians of Nebraska–his own people–La Flesche, then an ethnologist with the Smithsonian, received the degree of Doctor of Letters from the University of Nebraska on 2 July 1926.

He was born in a teepee on the Nebraska plains, was a graduate of the National University School of Law and was associated with the United States Bureau of Indian Affairs and the Smithsonian for 48 years. His greatest achievement was to rescue the language of the Osage tribe from oblivion, to which it seemed doomed after all the young people had begun to speak English.

THE ART AND FOLKLORE

Above: Jesse Cornplanter, descendant of Cornplanter, the famous Seneca chief, was photographed by Helen Post in July 1940 as he carved a ceremonial corn husk mask at the Tonawanda Community House in Tonawanda, New York. *(See page 25).*

Eastern North America is comprised of a dense woodland, stretching from the Atlantic coast to the Mississippi River and from the St Lawrence River Valley in Canada to the Gulf Coast. It is a region endowed with a changeable climate and a wide range of temperatures encompassing rocky coastlines, fertile coastal meadows and an abundance of mountains, rivers and streams that still support a rich variety of plant and animal life.

This area was occupied first by the mammoth hunters and then by small game hunters during the late Ice Age period from 10,000 to 7000 BC, when the climate was still harsh and inhospitable. Around 500 BC, a distinct woodland culture began to develop, and it reached its peak within 2000 years. By the middle of the sixteenth century, the native population in the region stood at over half a million.

Traditionally, the numerous Northeastern tribes had much in common. Primarily farmers and hunters, the men were superior warriors and women played key roles in daily life. Of all the tribes in North America, they were the most advanced politically, and many merged into confederations as a means of dealing with mutual problems. They were also united by language. The three major language groups were Iroquoian, Siouan and Algonquian, the latter incorporating the largest number of Indians and covering the most territory. Although they spoke many languages, the Indians in the Southeast were similar by virtue of their lifestyle.

The people of the region from the Atlantic coast to the western Mississippi Valley and from the Gulf of Mexico to Virginia and Kentucky lived in villages and were primarily agrarian. Unlike the Northeast, this area provided a mild climate, and, in addition, ample rainfall, lush and fertile land abundant in animal life and rivers and coastal waters full of fish. Prior to the arrival of the white man, the Indian population in the Southeast was divided between 150 and 200 diverse tribes, each with its own language and dialects. The Iroquoian-speaking Cherokee and Tuscarora lived in the northern ranges and were the most numerous peoples of the region. The Muskogean-speaking Choctaw, Chickasaw and Creeks were the dominant tribes farther south when the first Europeans arrived in the seventeenth century, by which time all of the Southeast cultures had reached their cultural peak of development. The

OF THE EASTERN TRIBES

Winnebago tribe in Wisconsin was the only member of the Siouan language family which prevailed on the Plains. The tribes had many accomplished craftsmen–good potters, basket weavers and stone workers.

In the North, the great Iroquoian culture evolved in the north during the fourteenth century, but consisted of a group of five hostile tribes. In upstate New York, between the Hudson Valley and Lake Erie, these tribes were involved in a constant state of war, trying to settle ever-increasing scores against each other. As with most Indians of North America, they were preoccupied with the art of warfare. In an effort to end this self-destruction and promote peace, Chief Hiawatha helped to create the League of Iroquois. Created around 1570, his confederation was made up of the five one-time antagonists: the Mohawks, Senecas, Oneidas, Onodagas and Cayugas. (The Tuscaroras joined in 1722.) By agreement, Iroquois territory was divided into five strips, with each tribe governing its territory by a council. Mutual problems and major issues were resolved by the Great Council, a body of 49 representatives from the five tribes, with the fiftieth seat reserved for Hiawatha.

The Iroquois community consisted of randomly arranged longhouses, one for each clan, with the clan crest painted above the door. The longhouse, a rectangular structure with an arched roof, was constructed of poles and sheets of bark. Inside, the walls were lined with two levels of bunks, one for sleeping and one for storing family possessions. Several fires were kept burning continuously. The Iroquois set up their villages at the forks of rivers or streams and erected a palisade, or a moat, for protection, with the fields for crops surrounding the village.

The Iroquois venerated a pantheon of supernatural beings, including spirits of plants, animals and natural forces. The magical force *Orenda*, for example, was the active power in every natural phenomenon, and could be invoked through ritual and magic. Ceremonies were a regular feature of Iroquois' lives, with many being extended, elaborate affairs. These ceremonies included chanting and singing, which were accompanied by drums, flutes and rattles. One of the most important was the four-day Great Corn Festival to give thanks for the corn harvest. During the week-long Ceremonial of

At Top: Nicholas Lolu, wife and child, of the Abnaki tribe. Photographed by John Bryson, July 1875.

Above: An abundance of lakes and rivers in the Subarctic made travel by water a major mode of transportation by the Native Americans. In this photograph by Roland Reed, Chippewa hunters, in their birchbark canoe, close in on their prey. One hunter propels and guides the canoe with the paddle made out of hard maple wood, while the hunter takes aim. The canoe also served as protection from the elements when turned upside down—a somewhat safe and warm place to sleep when not on the move.

Midwinter at year's end, the sacred fire from the old year was destroyed and replaced with a new one. At this time, individuals would recall the good signs that had appeared in their dreams during the year to provide guidance in the coming year.

Masks, which were portraits of mythological beings, were a spectacular feature of these ceremonies. Some masks were grotesque carvings from wood, and others were woven from corn husks. The Iroquois were famous for their False Face Society, named after the masked curers who healed the sick. Members of this group were summoned to perform rituals, wearing masks that possessed healing powers. The cured individual was then obliged to join the society. Among the Seneca, the largest of the Iroquoian tribes, was the Husk Face Society, a mask from which is pictured on these pages.

Although the Algonquian tribes were spread far and wide across the Northeast, they were considerably less powerful than the Iroquois. They were friendly and traded among themselves, but they were not united. In the far Northeast, Penobscot and Abnaki tribes lived a semi-nomadic life, contending with rough terrain and a hard climate, in the search for moose, their main source of food and clothing. The Algonquians, who lived around the Great Lakes in the most western reaches of the Northeast, relied heavily on a diet of wild rice. Maple sugar was also valuable. These semi-nomadic tribes returned to their villages in the summer to plant their crops. This was also the time of year for religious festivals honoring Manitou, the highest-ranking god. Summer was the season for war and for small-scale raids. However, young men were not permitted to go to war or to hunt until they had undertaken the Vision Quest. As with other tribes, this was the period of solitary fasting in the woods, waiting to receive the guardian spirit. The Midewiwin was a secret curing society peculiar to western Algonquians.

The Lenni-Lenape (the people) were typical of the Algonquian tribes that relied on farming for subsistence. Also known as the Delaware, they were a loose federation of small villages in which the men were the hunters, fishermen, warriors and healers and the women were the farmers, cooks and seamstresses, and responsible for rearing children. The Lenni-Lenape village was a haphazard arrangement of structures around a central big house, and living quarters were either rectangular buildings or small huts, with each village including a sweathouse for steam baths, the remedy for disease and melancholy. After cleansing themselves in the sweathouse, men repainted their bodies and women their faces with white, yellow and red dyes. Red was usually associated with war, because most men painted red designs on themselves before going into battle.

The extensive network of lakes and rivers that exists in Canada and those parts of the United States around the Great Lakes made travel by water a major mode of transportation by tribes of the area, and the Native Americans of this region became skilled boatmakers. Of all types of boats built in North America by the Indians, the umiak, kayak and birchbark canoe were superior in construction and quality. A variety of styles evolved, depending on the materials available in the local area. In the north, the predominant type was the birchbark canoe. This canoe was a versatile and sturdy piece of equipment. Strong but lightweight, it could be easily carried overground. Turned upside down it provided good protection from the elements, and on water it was essential for trading, hunting and general travel.

Building a canoe required about two weeks of intensive work, which was usually carried out in the springtime. The men cut the wood and the bark, while the women sewed. Bark was removed from white birch trees in huge sheets and sewn inside-out onto a white cedar frame with spruce or pine root 'threads' that were soaked in water for flexibility. Pine gum was heated and mixed with fat to seal the seams, and the floor was strengthened with cedar.

Politically, the tribes of the Northeast and the Southeast were the most highly organized north of Mexico, and many united in strong confederacies. Just as the Iroquois had their confederacy in the north near the Great Lakes, Creeks of the region that now comprises parts of Tennessee and Mississippi organized themselves into a federation of intertribal councils comprised of representatives from each community. The Southeastern tribes were organized according to the clan system, with chiefdom and kinship based on descent from the mother. Like the Iroquois, society was matrilineal, but men were the decision makers, and all business that affected the community was handled by councils of men.

Creek towns were laid out around a public square consisting of summer and winter council meeting buildings, a hot house for winter activities and a yard in one corner for sports and games. Houses were arranged in small groups around the square, with modest houses of the poorer families concentrated on the fringes of the village. The summer council meeting building was built with open sides, and the winter one with walls. They were rectangular buildings, with log frames and walls plastered with mud and grass. In the middle of the bark roof, a hole was left to allow for smoke to escape, since the sacred fires were kept burning continuously.

The Cherokee village was centered around a huge, seven-sided house that was dome shaped and made of earth. It was large enough to hold crowds of 500 for ceremonies and council meetings. Surrounding it were the games field and community farming land. On the edges of those fields there were small, rectangular buildings covered with clay and roofed with bark.

According to the folklore of the Southeast, the universe consisted of three separate worlds: the perfect Upper World, the unsettled Lower World and This World, and the realm in the middle. In their daily life, Indians strove to find a balance between the two extreme worlds and between good and bad forces. A large number of supernatural beings were revered by the people of this region, the most important of which was the Sun god, represented on Earth as fire. The main, sacred fire in the village was kept burning all year long and was used to light individual fires in each building. These were also kept burning throughout the year. Complicated rituals accompanied the planting and harvesting of crops. The Green Corn Dance was the year's most sacred holiday and took place when the corn ripened in the autumn, marking the end of the year. During this four- to eight-day ceremony, the sacred fire was destroyed and replaced with a new fire to symbolize a new year. Included in the ritual were fasting, feasting and bathing, as well as a thorough cleaning of all living areas.

By the early nineteenth century, white settlement had encroached heavily on the traditional lands of the Southeast tribes, and in 1830 the states of Mississippi, Alabama and Georgia prohibited any settlement by Native Americans within their borders. In spite of Chief Justice John Calhoun's strong defense of Indian rights in the Supreme Court, President Andrew Jackson pressed for passage of the Indian Removal Act, which in 1837 created Indian Territory west of the Mississippi in what is now Oklahoma as a home for all displaced Indians.

The Choctaws ceded their land in Mississippi and spent the next three years making their way to the land allocated to them in Arkansas and Oklahoma. The Cherokees in Georgia were pushed out by white settlers, and in return were given land in northeastern Oklahoma called Cherokee Strip. Those who refused to move were rounded up by General Winfield Scott and escorted west during the winter of 1838 and 1839. The 'Trail of Tears,' as this resettlement came to be called, took over 12 months to complete, and by the end of the long, arduous trek, one-quarter of the Indians had died. However, a small band of Cherokees were able to avoid the enforced migration and moved into North Carolina, where they bought land in the mountains and re-established a community and cultural tradition in isolation from white men and other members of the tribe.

The tribes that were first given land in Indian Territory were the five largest tribes from the Southeast: the Cherokee, Chickasaw, Choctaw, Creek and Seminole. These tribes quickly adopted many aspects of European culture, and as a result came to be referred to as the Five Civilized Tribes.

By 1887, so many tribes had been given land within Indian Territory that US government policy was changed, granting land to individual tribe members rather than to the tribe as a whole. By the time Oklahoma became a state in 1907, all of the Indian nations within Indian Territory had been dissolved. However, the people themselves stayed, and this area remains a major hub of Native American population, art and culture.

Notable places in the Northeast and Midwest where the artifacts of the ancient native art and culture of the region may be viewed today include: the Peabody Museum of Natural History at Yale University (New Haven, CT), Cahokia Mounds State Historical Site (Collinsville, IL), the University of Iowa Museum of Natural History (Iowa City), the Mille Lacs Indian Museum (Onamia, MN), the National Museum of the American Indian (New York City), the American Museum of Natural History (New York City), the Iroquois Indian Museum (Schoharrie, NY), the Seneca-Iroquois National Museum (Salamanca, NY), the Canadian Museum of Civilization (Hull, Quebec) and the Museum of Archaeology (Trois-Rivieres, Quebec).

Notable places in the Southeast where artifacts of the ancient native art and culture of the region may be viewed today include: the Florida Museum of Natural History (Gainsville), Etowah Indian Mounds State Historical Site (Cartersville, GA), the Grand Village of the Natchez (Natchez, MS), the Museum of the Cherokee (Cherokee, NC) and the Tennessee State Museum (Nashville). In addition, there are several important places in Oklahoma where Southeast culture is preserved. These include the State Museum of History (Oklahoma City) and the Gilcrease Museum (Tulsa). Visitors to Oklahoma may interact with contemporary Native American culture at the Cherokee Heritage Center (Tahlequah), the Choctaw Nation Capital (Tuskahoma), the Creek Council House (Okmulgee) and the American Indian National Hall of Fame (Anadarko).

THE CREATION OF THE HUMAN RACE (A Seneca Legend)

Note: Shagodyoweg Gowa is often translated as False Face, but the literal meaning is 'The Great One Who Protects Them (Mankind)' from sickness and pestilence, and is considered to be one of the Wind People.

A bove, in the center of the Blue, people lived before there was any earth down here. In the middle of the village up there stood a tree covered with white blossoms. When the tree was in bloom, its blossoms gave light to the people, and when the blossoms fell, there was darkness. One time, a woman in that village had a dream, and in her dream an *ongwe* (man) said to her, 'That tree with white blossoms on it must be pulled up by the roots.'

When the woman told her dream, the people were silent. Some time passed and the woman dreamed again.

The *ongwe* in her dream said, 'A circle must be dug around the tree and the tree pulled up by the roots. Then something giving more and better light will come.'

The woman told her dream a second time, but still the people took no heed of it. She dreamed a third time and again was told that the tree must be pulled up. Then a man said, 'I think we should give heed to this dream. We may have better light and the people will have cause to rejoice.' His advice was listened to, and men cut around the roots of the tree. When the roots were loosened, the tree sank down and disappeared.

The chief of the people said, 'I did not heed this dream for I knew something would happen to the people if the tree were pulled up.' He was angry and ordered that the woman, who had the dream should be brought and pushed into the hole left by the tree. Men caught her and threw her into the hole. Now that the tree with white blossoms was gone, it was dark all the time.

The woman fell and fell. The hole was deep and long, but at last she came out into bright light, into our sky, and, looking down, she saw only water.

It is well known that in very ancient days all animals had the gift of speech by which they communicated with one another as freely as human beings do at the present time.

Down under the Blue there was just one enormous body of water on which there were multitudes of various kinds of water fowl and aquatic animals amusing themselves after their own fashion. One of the duck family looked up and saw a dark object coming down from the sky.

The duck cried out to the other birds and animals, 'Some strange being is coming down to us!'

A council was called at once to decide how they could prepare a resting place for this being, who might not be fitted to live on the water as they did. A duck said, 'I'll dive and find if there is any bottom to this water.' After a time, the duck came to the surface, shot into the air and fell back, lifeless. Several other water birds made the same attempt with a similar result.

All the people that lived in the water were there.

Loon said to Fish-hawk, 'Go and meet that creature in the air and hold it till we are ready for you to come down.'

Fish-hawk went, and they saw him meet the woman–for it was a woman.

Turtle said, 'I'll take care of her.'

Loon said, 'You can't; you are too fond of eating.'

Horned Snake said, 'I'll take care of her. She can sit between my horns. I'll carry her wherever I go.'

Loon said, 'You can't care for her. You are poisonous; you would kill her.'

Meanwhile, one person after another was trying to bring earth from the bottom of the sea. At last Hell-diver brought up a little. Loon was chief, and when Hell-diver came up, he sent all that kind of people after more dirt.

Loon said, 'Put the dirt on Turtle's back.' Turtle was willing, and as fast as the divers brought dirt Beaver, with his tail, pounded it down on turtle's back to make it solid. When Loon thought there was enough dirt, Fish-hawk came down with the woman.

The Beaver and Duck people kept at work making the Earth larger and larger. As it grew, more Beavers and Ducks were ordered to work. Bushes began to grow, little red bushes like water reeds.

Soon the woman gave birth to a child, a girl. The child quickly grew to be a young woman and to be very active. She walked here and there and watched the birds and animals, and once, when she was wandering around, she met a nice-looking young man. They fell in love with each other, and by their union came night and day. At daybreak, the young woman went to meet her husband; at twilight she went home and the man went away.

One evening, after they had parted, the young woman turned to look at her husband and saw a Turtle walking along where the man had just been. She thought, 'A Turtle has deceived me!'

She told her mother about the man and said, 'I am going to die. You must put my body in the ground and cover it up well. Two stalks will grow from my breasts, and on each stalk an ear of corn will come. When the ears are ripe, you must pick them and give one to each of the boys that are born to me.'

The younger woman gave birth to twin boys, and died. The mother buried her daughter, and soon two stalks came up out of her grave. And this was the origin of corn.

The boys grew quickly. They were strong and healthy, but the younger one was an awkward, ugly-looking, disagreeable fellow with a head like a lump of rough flint. Once, when the elder brother was off by himself, he was lonesome and he thought he would try to make something. So he took mud, and when he had molded it into the shape he wanted, he put it down and asked, 'Can't you jump?'

The creature didn't move, so he blew on it till at last it jumped. He had created the grasshopper. Then he thought he would make something that would fly higher, so of red clay he made the cherry bird. After he had the clay molded, he set it up and told it to fly in the air. The bird flew and lighted on a bough; this was the first bird. One after another, he made all of the birds of the air.

Then he thought he would make something that would run on the ground, so he shaped a deer, brought it to life and said to it, 'You must run fast and go everywhere in the world.' He blew on it and pushed it, and it ran off. In the same way he made different kinds of animals.

Then he thought, 'Maybe I can make something like myself.' Out of the mud he made something that looked like himself. But now, in some way, he found that he had a spirit in his body, and he wanted the thing he had lying on the ground to have a spirit too. He wanted to give it some of his own but didn't know how. At last, he bent down and blew into its mouth. He hadn't blown into the mouth of any other creature he had made. The image began to move. The young man raised it up, made it stand on its feet and told it to whoop.

The new man whooped; he had a fine voice. Then he walked off a little way and turned and looked at the young man.

The elder brother had a special place to sit when he made all these creatures. About the time he made man, the younger brother found the place and, while watching his brother he thought, 'I will make make a man too.' He went away alone, made something as nearly like himself as he could and brought it to life. It didn't look like a man. It was a strange creature, and when its maker saw that it wasn't a man but some ugly, deformed thing, he said to it, 'My brother has made a man. He is over there. Go and kill him.'

The elder brother was watching the younger, for he was afraid he would make some harmful animal. When he heard him tell the creature he had made to go and destroy man, he went back to his own place, caught cherry bird, and, pulling out the hind leg of grasshopper, gave it to the bird and said, 'Go and scare my brother.'

As the bird took up the leg, the bird became very large and the leg was like the leg of a man, and it was bloody. The bird flew near, perched on a limb and called out, '*Gowa*! *Gowa*!'

When the younger brother saw what the bird had in its beak, he left his work, ran home and said to his grandmother, 'A bird came and perched just where I was at work. My brother made it to frighten me. I was afraid it would pull my leg out, so I ran.'

When the elder brother came, the grandmother said, 'You shouldn't frighten your brother.'

The first man made was wandering about alone. The young man saw him once in a while and saw that he was lonesome. Then he said to himself, 'I will make something like my grandmother.' He made it out of mud, breathed into it and told it to walk. Then he found the man and said, 'I give you this one. You must always go together.'

When the woman sat down by the man, he thought that her arm was in the way and his was also. He said, 'We will cut them off.' They cut them off and laid them to one side.

When the elder brother came along and saw what they had done, he said to himself, 'This won't do. I will give them blood and pain.' And from himself he gave them blood and pain. Then he put their arms back on and healed them. Before this, they had neither blood nor pain.

To the man and woman he said, 'I have made you. You will have children like yourselves. You must hunt the animals I have made, kill them and eat their flesh; that will be your food. I am going above the Blue. You will not live forever. You will die and your spirit will go above the Blue.'

When the younger brother found that the elder brother had gone away, he saw the man and woman and talked with them. He said, 'I am going to make a man.' He got earth and formed it as best he could, blew into its mouth and told it to stand up and whoop. It said, 'Ho, ho!' He pushed it from behind and made it leap. It was a frog, as large as a man.

The younger brother was angry and he said, 'I can't make a man. My brother has made a man and a woman and other animals. What I have made shall turn to man-eaters and animal eaters and will eat up what my brother has made.'

When the elder brother looked down from the Blue and saw that the animals his brother had made were trying to eat up the people and animals he had made, he came down, put the man-eaters in the ground and told them to stay there as long as the Earth remained. This work done, he went back to the Blue.

When the younger brother found that his animals were in the ground, he was angry and said, 'I will try again to make a man.' He got mud and began. Every little while, he went and looked at the man his brother had made. When his man was finished and brought to life, he was an ugly-looking creature. His maker told him to whoop. He could only say 'Ho, ho!' And this was Shagodyoweg Gowa. His maker said, 'Go and eat all the creatures my brother has made.'

When the elder brother saw what was taking place, he came from the Blue to put Shagodyoweg into the ground, but that one spoke first and said, 'Do not destroy me. I want to live on the Earth. I will be your servant and help you. I will go around in the woods. The ashes of fire will be my medicine for men. If anyone is sick, I will take ashes and scatter them over him and he will be well.'

The elder brother couldn't put Shagodyoweg into the ground, for he had spoken first, so he let him stay on Earth.

The younger brother said to his grandmother, 'I have tried to make a man, but I cannot. Now I will cause the people my brother has made to do all manner of evil.'

The elder brother went back to the Blue.

SUMMER KILLS AUTUMN AND IS HERSELF KILLED BY WINTER (A Seneca Legend)

Note: Dagwanoenyent is the Whirlwind or Cyclone, always represented as an immense head. Shagodiaqdane is the Woman in the South. Shagodyoweg Gowa is the God of the Air (the Wind People).

There was a man called Donwenwa who wouldn't let anyone come into his house. He had two nephews old enough to hunt small game: birds, squirrels and coons. The boys lived in a house near their uncle's, and each morning he called to them saying, 'Up, boys! or the game will be gone.' The boys jumped up and were off.

One day, the younger boy heard something making a noise. He listened and listened and at last found that the noise came from the ground. He ran to his brother and said, 'Come and help me dig. I hear a noise down in the ground.'

The brother went to the place with him and they began to dig with sharp sticks. When they got down some distance, they found a hollow and in it a little child.

'This is the best luck we've had yet,' said the elder boy. 'This will be our brother, but I'm afraid our uncle will find out about him. If he does, he'll kill him and eat him.'

'We'll try to save him. We'll fix it so our uncle won't find him,' said the younger boy.

They carried the child home. That night, the uncle woke up, stretched himself and said, 'I think my nephews have found game; I hear it breathing. I'll go and ask them.' He stuck his head in at their door and asked, 'Well, boys, have you any game?'

'No,' answered the younger brother.

'I hear it breathing.'

'How can you tell? There are two of us here.'

'I hear three breathing.'

'If you know there are three, you may as well kill us.'

'Our people don't allow a man to kill his nephews.'

'Well, you'll not kill our brother,' said the younger nephew. 'If you kill him, you must kill us.'

The old man went home, but came back and stuck his head in the door again. 'You might as well give me that boy,' said he.

'If you kill him, you'll kill us,' answered the elder nephew.

When the old man found that his nephews wouldn't give him the child, he promised not to harm it.

All went well for a time. Then the younger brother said, 'I think we had better go away and leave our uncle.'

'We can't leave him,' said the elder.

'Why can't we?'

'He would follow us.'

'We can try to get away. We are not safe here.'

They gathered dry sticks and piled them up near the house. Then one morning they set the sticks on fire, and, running around on the house top, they jumped into the smoke, and it carried them up and away.

After a while, they came to the ground and hid under a big stone.

That night Donwenwa thought the boys were very quiet. He went to their house, stuck his head in and found that they were gone.

'Oh, my poor nephews,' he said. 'They think they can get away from me.'

He tracked them to the top of the house and found that they jumped into the blaze and went off in the smoke. Then he went straight to the stone where they were and struck the stone with a *dadishe* (a sort of cane). The stone split open and he found the three boys.

'Come out, boys,' he said. 'We'll go home. You should stay at home, not try to go away from me.'

When the boys were back in their own house, the second brother asked, 'Haven't we any relatives except this old man?'

'We have,' said the elder brother. 'We have another uncle worse looking and crosser than this one, and we have aunts.'

'Can't we go and see our uncle?'

'We can, but we must ask this uncle how to go.'

The younger brother went to the old man, struck him with a mallet and said, 'I want you to tell me how I can go and see my uncle in the East.'

'You have no uncle in the East.'

'Yes, I have.'

'You have no uncle there, or if you have, he is very cross. He is Hatdedases, the Whirlwind Maker. He'll kill us all if he comes here. But you can go and see him if you are able to draw a bow that I will make for you.'

The old man made a strong bow and a big double-headed arrow, and told his nephew to try it. The elder brother took the bow first and couldn't bend it. The younger brother bent it easily. Then the uncle gave him the arrow and, pointing to a great hickory tree, said, 'Shoot that.'

He shot and the arrow split the tree.

Then the old man said, 'That will do. You many go and try to see your Uncle Dagwanoenyent (or Hatdedases). If he sees you before you shoot him, he'll say "*Ogongahgeni*," and fly off. If you succeed in shooting him before he sees you, pick up the arrow and shoot again. Then he'll ask you what you want and you'll answer, 'I want you to come and live with us. We'll give you plenty of rocks and hickory sticks to eat and make you a nest to lie in.'

The boy started, and after traveling a long distance came to a place where he heard a great cracking and gnawing noise. He called his medicine mole and told it to make a trail under the ground to the place the noise came from so he could follow the trail.

Dagwanoenyent stopped gnawing and listened; the mole stopped. The old man gnawed again; the mole went on. A second time the old man stopped and listened; the mole stopped. And so it went on until the mole was straight in front of Dagwanoenyent. Then the mole made a hole and the boy came to the top of the ground, drew his bow and hit his uncle in the middle of the forehead. The arrow rebounded; he caught it and shot again. The third time he shot, Dagwanoenyent called out, 'I give up. What do you want?'

'I want you to come and live with us. We'll give you plenty of rocks and hickory sticks to eat and a good nest to live in. If you don't come. I'll shoot you again.'

Dagwanoenyent said, 'Go and fix the nest and gather rocks and sticks for me to eat, and I'll come.'

The boy went home, and he and his brother and uncle put up a strong platform, and on top of it, they made a nest. When all was ready, the old man came and settled on the nest.

Once, when the two boys were out hunting, the younger boy heard a noise off in the South. While he stood listening, a False Face ran toward him. The boy was frightened. He darted around trees and tried to get away. At last, when he was getting tired, he called loudly, '*Haknosen* Donwenwa *gadjionegaq-dianh*.' ('Donwenwa, if you don't come, I shall be killed.')

That minute, Donwenwa was there saying, 'I'll save you.' He struck False Face with his *onwe* and killed him.

After a time, the elder nephew thought he would go toward the South and see if anything would happen to him. When he had traveled a long distance, he heard someone singing, and, going toward the voice through the dense woods, he came to an opening, and at the farther end of the opening saw the singer. Her song said, 'A young boy is coming for me. He has no power; he can't come where I am.'

When the boy heard this, he was angry and said, 'She isn't strong enough to keep me back. I'll go there and pound her.'

He doubled up his fist and ran toward the woman. She didn't look up and kept on singing. When he came to where she was sitting, he struck her a heavy blow, but instead of falling over, she said, 'Ha, ha! Who touches me?' That minute, the boy fell to the ground dead.

The woman straightened out the body and talked to it, saying, 'Poor boy, you thought you could kill me. Now you are dead,' She pushed the body a little to one side and kept on singing.

When the boy didn't come home, his brother went to hunt for him. He tracked him till he came to where he had stood and listened to the singing. He heard the same song, and, looking across the opening, saw the woman and his brother's body. He was angry, and, doubling up his fist, he ran across the opening and struck the woman a heavy blow on her head.

'Ha, ha! Who touches me?' she growled. That minute, the boy fell to the ground, dead. She straightened out the body and kept on singing.

The third boy–the boy the brothers had dug out of the ground–went to look for the other two and was killed as they had been.

That night, Donwenwa wondered why he heard no breathing at the other house and wondered if the boys had run away again. Going to the house, he stuck his head in, and, seeing no one, said, 'They can't get away from me! I'll find them, wherever they are.'

The next morning, he went toward the South till he came to the place where the boys had stood and listened to the woman's song. When he saw the woman and the three bodies he said, 'You've killed my nephews. Now I'll kill you!'

Running to the woman, he gave her a terrible blow, and, before she had a chance to say anything, he gave her a second and a third blow. But then she got a chance to call out, 'Ha, ha! Who touches me?' and that instant, the old man grew weak and died.

Now Dagwanoenyent missed his brother and nephews. 'My brother,' said he, 'thinks that he has great power, but he hasn't. Maybe he has been killed by that woman in the South. I'll go and find him.'

He followed the tracks of his nephews and brother till he came to the clearing and saw the woman sitting on the ground singing. He flew at her and struck such a heavy blow that she had no chance to speak. He hit her a second and third blow. Then his hair began to fall out–his strength was in his long hair–but he kept striking. The woman had no chance to speak and at last he killed her. Then he called to his brother and nephews. 'Get up. You ought to be ashamed to lie there.'

The four came to life and went home. They lived on quietly for a while. Then the younger brother said that he was going to travel around the world and see what he could find, and he started off toward the East. After traveling some distance, he saw a hut, and, going into it, found an old, blind man and began to torment him.

The old man said, 'My brothers will come soon and then you'll stop abusing me.'

The boy thought he would go before the other men came. He spent the night under a tree, and the next day he traveled till nearly sundown, and then came to a house. There was an old man in the house who said, 'I'm glad you have come. I want to gamble with plum stones.'

'What will you bet?' asked the boy.

'I always bet heads. If you beat me, you'll cut off my head; if I beat you, I'll cut off your head.'

The old man had a stone bowl and some plum stones. The boy threw first and lost. Then the old man threw and lost. But in the end the boy won, and he cut off the old man's head, and then traveled on.

Soon he saw a wasp's nest hanging from the limb of a tree. He stopped up the hole in the nest, and, cutting off the limb, carried it along with him in a bundle. He hadn't gone far when he saw a great many people coming toward him. He wanted to pass them, but they caught hold of him and said, 'You are only a boy. We are going to kill you.'

'You must wait awhile,' said the boy. 'When anyone is going to be killed, it is the custom to let him do something first.' He put down his bundle and said, 'Tear it open if you want to.'

They snatched up the bundle and tore it open. The wasps flew at them, and in the excitement, they forgot the boy, who ran off as fast as he could. This time he ran toward home. When he came in sight of his uncle's house, things looked strange. He didn't see Dawanoenyent's nest. Then he found that his uncles and brothers were gone.

He searched for tracks, and, finding none, he began to mourn. And he mourned till at last he changed into a red fox.

The woman in the South was Summer, the boys Autumn and old Cyclone, and he who at last conquered her was Winter.

SUMMER CONQUERS WINTER (A Seneca Legend)

Note: Nyagwaithe Gowa is the Ancient of Bears. Génonskqa is a 'Stone Coat' (Ice and Great Cold).

There was a village where it was the habit of the people to fight a great deal; they were warlike. A boy came to that village. He was perhaps four years old. No one knew where he came from. He wandered around staying here and there. First one family kept him awhile, then another. The people didn't care for the child or pay much attention to him.

One spring, when the boy was almost a young man, there was a good deal of talk about getting up a party to go on the warpath. Twenty men volunteered. The boy wanted to go. He asked one man and another, but all refused. Then he said, 'I will go anyhow.'

The 20 men started out and the boy went with them. When night came, fires were built and two men camped at each fire. The boy built his own fire and sat by it alone.

Several days passed. One night the boy had a dream. A man appeared to him and said, 'If you keep on in the direction you are going, you will all perish tomorrow at midday. Tell the head man of the party and ask him to change his course.'

They were going south.

When the boy told his dream to the leader of the party, he was angry and said to his men, 'I didn't want this fellow to come. He is a hindrance and a coward. We have come to meet an enemy. Why should we turn back even if we knew there was one on our road?'

After eating, they went on, paying no heed to the boy's dream.

When the Sun was near the middle of the sky, the boy, who was in the rear–the party was going Indian file–noticed that the leader stopped, then the next man stopped and the next. When he came up, he found they were looking at a track.

'It is Nyagwaithe,' said the leader. 'The bear that kills everyone it meets. It knows when a person looks at its track, and no matter how far away it is, it comes back and destroys that person.'

The boy listened, and then said, 'I would like to see this bear.'

The men said, 'No you wouldn't. Nobody wants to see such a terrible creature.' But the boy insisted.

Then the leader said, 'If you want to see the bear, you mustn't follow us. We will turn off here and you can keep on, but if you meet it and run, don't run in the direction we take.'

They urged him to go with them, but he wouldn't.

The boy hung his bundle in the crotch of a tree, then went on, and soon, not far ahead, he saw something of enormous size. When nearer, he found it was a great bear and that it sat up on the trail with its back toward him. He crept close and looked at the creature. It had no hair on its body except a little at the end of its tail. He sent an arrow. The bear sprang forward, then turned and ran after him. It got so near that he could feel its breath.

The boy dodged from tree to tree, and then darted off and ran swiftly, the bear close behind. He came to a stream that was deep but narrow. He jumped across it. The bear followed him.

The boy sprang back and the bear sprang back. The boy jumped across the stream a number of times, with the bear always just behind him.

The boy felt his strength increasing; the bear's strength was failing. To tire the bear, the boy made a great circle before he sprang. At last, the bear fell behind; as it sprang across the stream, the boy passed it coming back. Soon the bear had to scramble to get a footing on the bank. The boy shot and the arrow entered the middle of one of the bear's forefeet. The bear scrambled on the bank, reeled from tree to tree, staggered, fell, rose again, struggled for a time, and then rolled over and died.

The boy took three hairs from the bear's whiskers and one tooth from its jaw. He went back to where he had left his bundle, took it, followed the trail of the 20 men, ran fast, overtook them and said, 'I have killed the Nyagwaithe you were so afraid of.'

They were astonished, for no man had ever killed a Nyagwaithe. They said, 'If he has done this, he must have great power. Let us go and see.'

They traveled till sundown, and then came to where the bear lay and saw it was of immense size. They said, 'We'll build a fire and burn the body. Then each man can take some of the ashes and a bone for medicine to give him power.'

Towards morning, when the fire had burned down, they stirred the ashes till each man found a bone. The leader said, 'You must be careful about taking up the remnants of this bear. Let each man, before he takes up his bone, say what gift he wants, what power.'

Most of the men wished to be good hunters and brave warriors; some wished to be fast runners. The tooth and whiskers were good for every purpose, so the boy didn't tell the men that he had taken anything. They had changed their ideas of him. They now looked on him as having great power.

The party traveled many days, camping at night. One night, the young man had a dream and the dream said, 'Tomorrow you will meet an enemy of greater number then your own party. Among them is a large man of immense power. He is so much larger than the rest of the men that you will easily know him. You must all fight him. When you meet the enemy, let every man hang up his bundle and begin to fight.'

The young man didn't tell his dream. After eating, the party traveled on. When the Sun was well up, they saw a bear on the trail ahead. It got up, stretched itself and looked at them.

When they came nearer the bear said, 'We have met and we shall get what we want.' Then he turned and disappeared. The bear was one of the enemy's men, sent to challenge the opponent.

The leader said to his men, 'Our enemy is near. Be of good courage. We will conquer.'

They went on and before long saw the enemy. The enemy saw them and gave a war whoop, and arrows began to fly.

The young man said, 'Let every man hang his bundle on a tree.'

They hung up their bundles and began to fight.

The young man remembered his dream and looked for the large warrior. When he saw him, he saw that he had a medicine that he held in front of his face to ward off arrows. This defense was larger than the one the young man had–the smaller it was, the more power it possessed–and the young man felt sure of success, as Stone Coats (Ice and Cold) were born with this power, a tiny hand to be kept on the palm of the hand. The young man was a Stone Coat.

The large man said, 'You will get what you deserve. You Stone Coat, I will kill you.'

He and the young man watched out, each eager to kill the other. They paid no attention to the rest of the warriors. They fought with clubs. At last, the young man snatched his opponent's club, hurled it away and threw him down.

When the enemy saw their leader overpowered, they ran. The big warrior and many of his party were killed. The Northern men piled up the dead and burned them. They had secured a long string of scalps.

When the party went back to the village and told what had happened, the young man was made chief. They thought him a Stone Coat, though he didn't look like one.

Another expedition was arranged. Many volunteered, but only 30 were chosen. They went South, as before. The third night, the young chief dreamed that a man came to him and said, 'Tomorrow night when you camp an enemy will camp nearby, and you will discover each other. [It was not the custom of Indians to attack in the night; they waited till daylight.] Be sure that you make the attack.'

The next morning when the chief told his dream, the men believed him. That night they discovered the enemy not far away. Toward daylight, the chief told his men to be ready. Just as light came, they started. As they stole near, they saw that the enemy was preparing for an attack.

The chief said to his warriors, 'We will circle around the camp. When around, I will raise a war whoop. Then let every man whoop and attack.'

The chief saw that one of the enemy's warriors was a much larger man than the others and he had a medicine shield to ward off arrows that was about the size of his own. Then he said to his men, 'You must fight desperately. I don't know how this will end.'

The big warrior shouted, 'You are among these men, are you, Stone Coat? I am going to kill you.'

The chief didn't hold up his medicine shield.

When the two met, they used their clubs first, and then they grappled. The chief, getting a good hold of the big man, pulled out his arm and threw it off. Right away it was back. Then the big man pulled off the chief's arm and hurled it away. In an instant, it was back and was as before.

While the two fought, the shouting and noise began to die away. Once in a while there was a shout, but it could be known that many people were being killed.

The chief pulled off the man's head, tore off the flesh and kicked away the pieces as they came back, for if the pieces were kept away till cold, their strength died and they couldn't come back. He kept the pieces away till the big man died.

When the fight was over and their enemy conquered, the chief found that 15 of his men had been killed. Those left went back to their village and for a long time there was no more fighting.

When the chief had passed the prime of life he said, 'I am getting old. I want to go on one more expedition. Then I will be satisfied.'

Forty men volunteered. They went toward the South, for the people they were to fight with came from the South. One night, the chief dreamed that a man appeared and said, 'I have come to tell you that a very powerful man will be with the enemy. Maybe you will not be able to conquer him. Tomorrow, just before midday, an owl will light on your trail and say, "Be ready. The enemy is near."'

In the morning, the chief told his dream. At midday they heard an owl hoot. It flew along the trail, lighted on a tree and said, 'The enemy is near.'

The chief said to his men, 'Be ready! Hang your bundles on a tree. If the big man throws me twice, you had better run.'

While they were hanging up their bundles, they heard the enemy's war whoop. When they were near, the men of the South called out, 'We have come to destroy you. You have destroyed our other expeditions. Now we will destroy you.'

The chief and the strong man met and fought with clubs. Then they threw down their clubs and clinched. They struggled for a time and the chief was thrown, but he sprang up and threw the strong man, who had barely touched the ground when he was up again.

The second time the chief was thrown, his men ran off some distance, then turned and looked back. The chief was up again. They saw his arm pulled off; it was on again. Then his head was hurled away. Some of the men ran toward home, but five hid and remained.

The enemy began to gather up the dead. They thought all of the chief's men had run away. The chief was dead. The men in hiding saw the enemy gather up his limbs and flesh. Then they heard the strong man say, 'We will hold a council and give thanks for conquering this man who has killed so many of our people.'

They formed a ring and placed in the center the pieces of the chief's body.

They were to give thanks by singing a war song. A man sang, and as he sang, he went towards the chief's feet. When the song ended, the singer went to the chief's head and said, 'You have been conquered. Now we will have peace,' and he struck the head with his club saying, 'I will punish you.'

That instant, the pieces flew together and became the chief again. He sprang up, killed five men, then lay down and fell apart.

The Southern people said, 'Our singer did wrong to abuse a warrior after he was dead. This is why we have lost five men. We had better kill him before he brings us more bad luck.'

They cut off the singer's head, and then sang the war song over, but no one raised a club or other weapon.

Of the chief's men, 10 out of the 40 reached home. They said, 'The friend whom we depended upon is dead. We must stay at home hereafter.'

This was a battle between Winter and Summer, and Summer prevailed. The tribe lived in peace after that.

THE GREAT SPIRIT OVERPOWERS THE COLD AND FROST OF WINTER (A Seneca Legend)

In the old time when men got lost while hunting, it was supposed the Winter God (Stone Coat) ate them.

Once three Senecas started off on the warpath, going toward the West. At night, they camped in a deep ravine at the head of a stream. After they had made a fire, a fine-looking man came and said to them, 'I think it is right to do what I am going to do. I have come to tell you that there are many people, man-eaters, on the warpath. Tonight they will make their camp in sight of yours. One of you must go to their fire and say "Hallo! I've found your fire. Where are you going?" And they will answer, "We are on the warpath." The man must say, "I am on the warpath too." They will say, "Well, we will fight." Then the man must leave them and come back to your camp.'

The stranger disappeared, and soon people came and camped a short distance from the Seneca camp. One of the three Senecas said, I will go over there.'

As he approached, he called out, 'Hallo! I've found your fire! Where are you going?'

'We are on the warpath.'

'So am I,' answered the Seneca.

'Well, we must fight,' said the chief of the Stone Coats.

As the man turned to go away, he saw stone clothing leaning against a tree; the owner of the clothes was lying on the ground.

The next morning, the Stone Coat warriors came up the ravine toward the Seneca camp. They made a terrible noise, for they sang, 'We are going to eat up the Seneca nation! We are going to eat up the Seneca nation!'

When they were about half way through the ravine, they gave a war whoop and moved forward quickly. But at that moment, huge rocks began to roll down on them and great trees began to fall on them. The Senecas saw a strange man running along on top of the rocks and trees. Whenever he saw a Stone Coat head sticking up, he struck it and killed the man.

Of all the warriors, only one was left alive, and he was never seen again. All the time the stranger was throwing rocks and trees, he sang, and the song said that the Seneca nation could stand against anything, could stand against the whole world.

When the battle was over, the stranger came to the three men and said, 'I am he whom you call Haweniyo (Great Spirit). I have saved you. I did not make the Stone Coats; someone else made them. I want you, the Seneca people, to be the most active of all tribes in war, in games and in hunting.'

The stranger disappeared and the three Senecas went home.

One day, a Seneca, who was out hunting in the woods, saw that a Stone Coat was following him. He was frightened and began to run. When he saw that the Stone Coat was gaining on him, he climbed a tree that had fallen part way and lodged on another tree.

The Stone Coat came to the tree and stopped but he couldn't see the man for he couldn't look up. Taking a finger from his pocket, he placed it on the palm of his hand. The finger raised up and pointed at the man.

The man was a swift runner. He slipped down from the tree, snatched the finger and ran off with it. Stone Coat shouted after him, begged and promised to be his friend forever if he would give him back the finger. The man, afraid of being deceived, wouldn't go near the Stone Coat, but he threw the finger back to him.

Ever after this, this man and the Stone Coats were good friends.

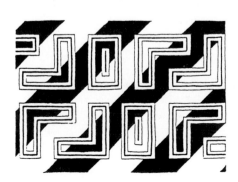

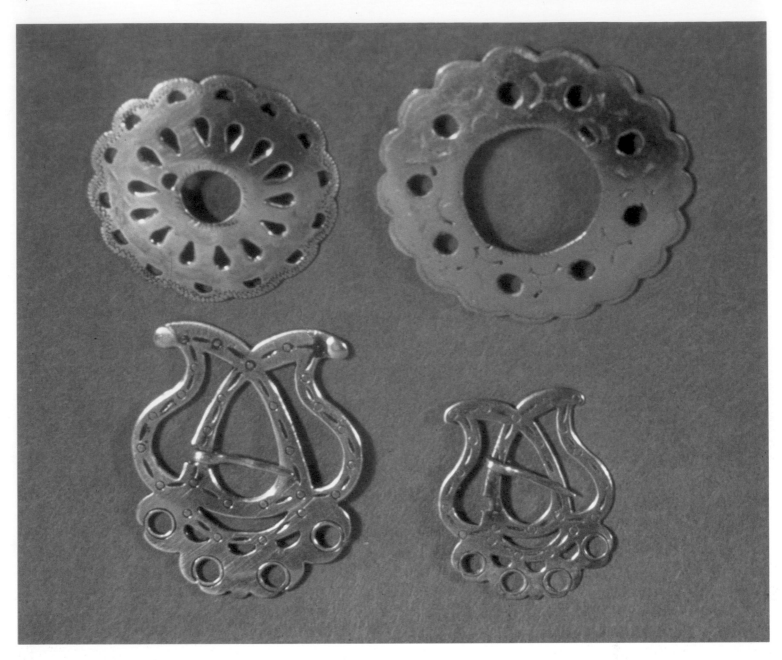

Jewelry
Iroquois, eighteenth century
(Cut and hammered metal)

Kneeling Cougar
Muskogean, sixteenth century
(carved wood)

This anthropomorphic feline figure is a relic from an ancient site at Key Marco (now Marco Island) off the west coast of Florida. At the end of the nineteenth century, archaeologist Frank Hamilton Cushing discovered by chance a large number of artifacts on this otherwise deserted island. The figure shown here is six inches tall and was carved with tools made of sharks' teeth. When the carving was completed, it was covered with a protective greasy coating.

Other carvings discovered include masks and numerous small animal figures, some of which were made with movable parts. Muskogeans made excellent use of the materials at hand, especially the large supply of shells washed up by the sea, which they turned into tools or used to decorate carvings.

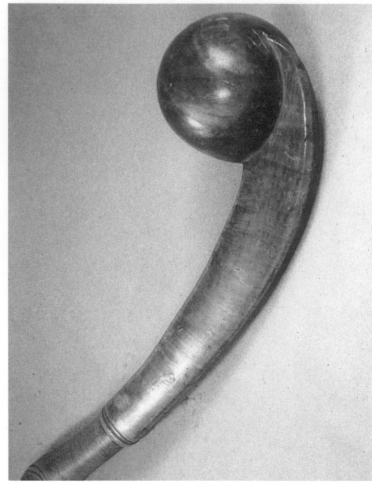

Plaited Basket
Chitimacha, early twentieth century
(dried cane)

This basket is a product of the Chitimacha, who lived at the mouth of the Mississippi River. In basket making, a variety of materials, including reeds, roots, bark and grasses, were woven by plaiting, coiling or twining to produce an enormous assortment of shapes and designs. Decoration was applied by means of vegetable dye or by incorporating feathers, shells, beads, quills or buckskin.

In the Southeast, dried cane was usually used, and it was woven by a technique called twilled plaiting. The warp and weft are identical in size and shape in plaited baskets, resulting in a very angular design characteristic of Southeastern basketry. Natural cane was either green or yellow, and black and red vegetable dyes from walnut and oak bark, respectively, completed the color range and were used for decoration.

Club
Iroquois, eighteenth century
(carved wood)

Corn Husk Mask
Seneca, early twentieth century
(corn husk)

Members of the Husk Face Society, a small religious group, traditionally wore these masks and danced during the Midwinter Ceremonial when they prophesied plentiful crops. The mask is made almost entirely of corn husks, braided and sewn together. The nose is wood or husk. To many Eastern tribes, corn was the most important crop, and many ceremonies were felt to be necessary to ensure a proper harvest.

Effigy Pipe (Fox)
Middle Woodlands Culture, 150 BC-200 AD
(carved catlinite, 2.5″ × 8.25″ × 4.5″)

Staff Decoration of Human/Alligator
Seminole (?), nineteenth century
(carved wood)

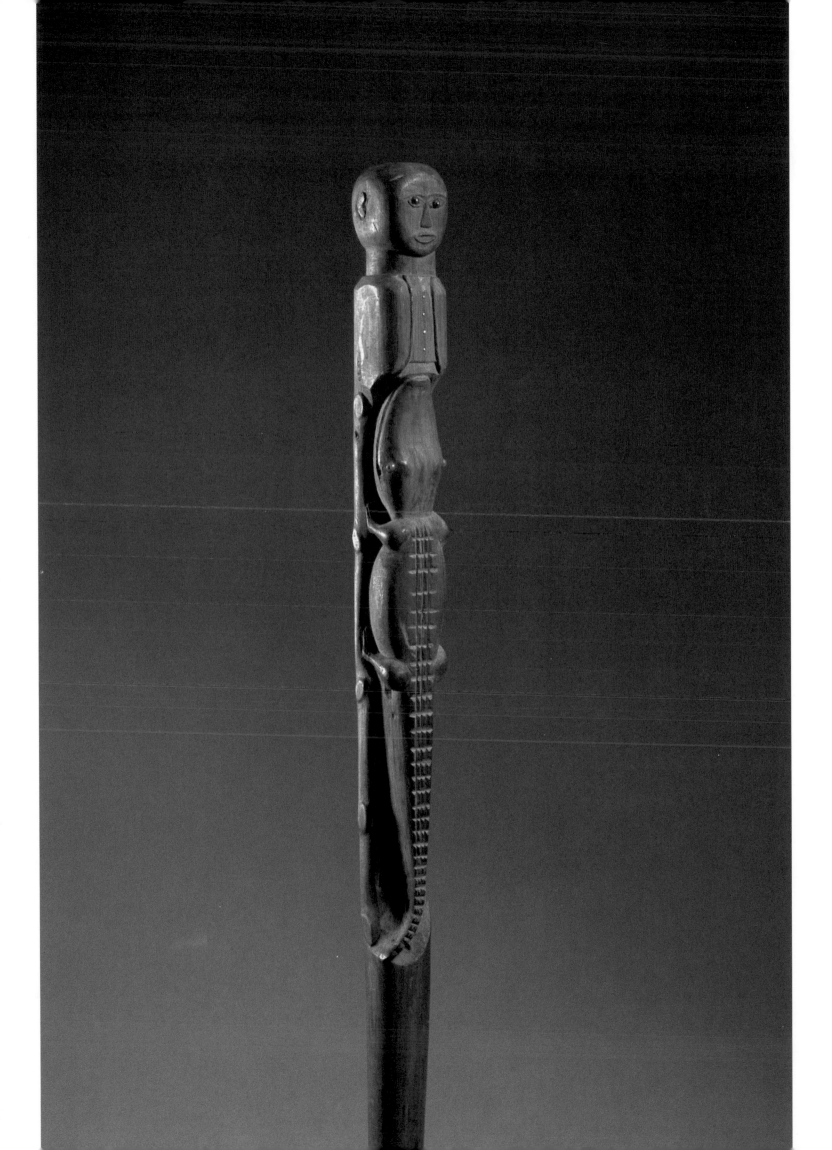

Face Mask
Iroquois, eighteenth century
(carved hardwood with metal fittings)

Case Used for Packing Provisions or Clothing
Ponca, eighteenth century
(painted parfleche)

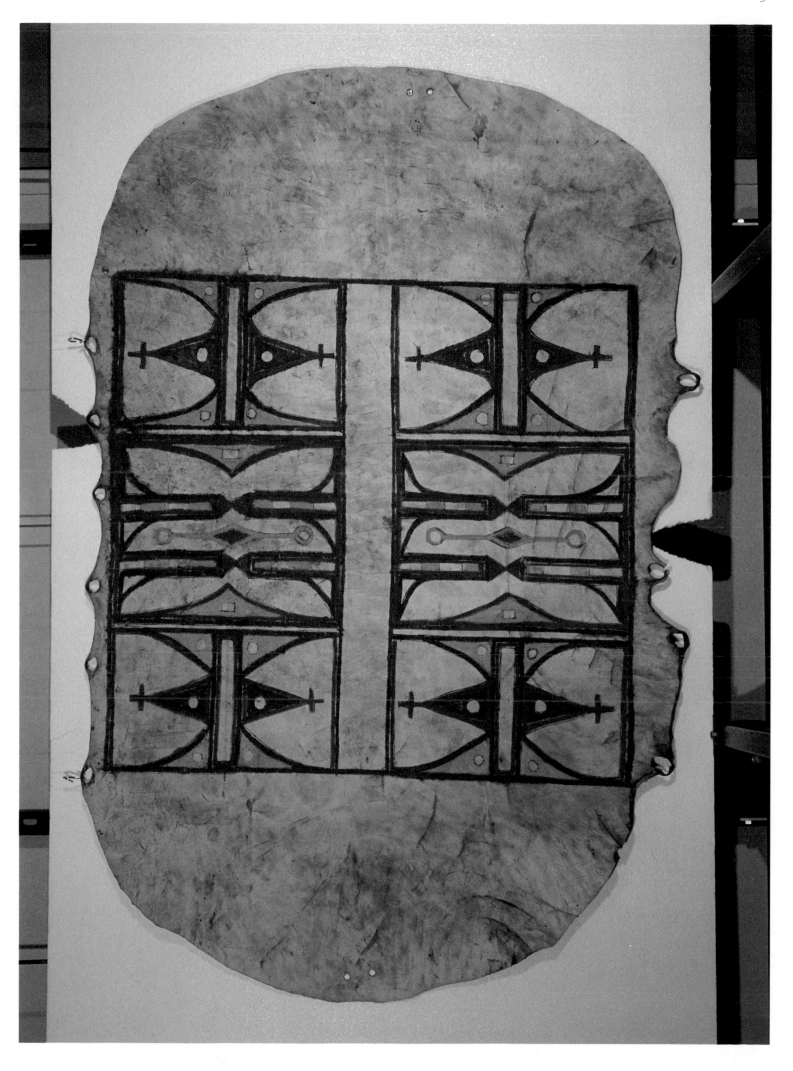

Scared Gray Wolf
Dorothy Strait (Cherokee), 1986
(oil, 36″×48″)

Dorothy Strait is a fifth generation Cherokee artist from Stillwell, OK. She learned techniques in oils and watercolors at an early age from her mother and grandfather, and later studied with Burdell Moody at Scottsdale, AZ. Strait now paints her native people in their ceremonials, legends and everyday life. She has had many prestigious exhibitions, art shows and one-woman shows, and is the 1988 winner of the Inter-tribal Indian Ceremonial Poster Award at Gallup, NM.

Shawl and Blanket
Shalah Rowlen (Sac & Fox and Pawnee), 1982
(ribbonwork-appliqué)

Sac & Fox Moccasins
Shalah Rowlen (Sac & Fox and Pawnee), 1982
(ribbonwork on tanned deer hide)

Shalah Rowlen's work has been shown at the Southern Plains Indian Museum and Crafts Center (Anadarko, OK), the Native American Center for the Living Arts (Turtle Museum, Niagara, NY), the National Museum of the American Indian (New York City) and the Eiteljorg Museum of the American Indian and Western Art (Indianapolis, IN).

Two Stars Falling
SS Burrus (Cherokee), 1989
(painted gourd)

Red Bear Gourd
SS Burrus (Cherokee), 1989
(painted gourd)

Winter Shaman
Reuben Kent (Kickapoo/Iowa/Oto), 1990
(raku and mixed media, 17.5″×11″)

With Dignity
Diana Beach (Cherokee), 1991
(colored pencil, 18.25″ × 24.25″)

Hummingbird Beaded Hat
Char Pully (Penobscot), 1991
(glass beads, felt top hat, feathers)

Rug-Blanket
Nowetah Timmerman (Susquehanna-Cherokee), 1987
(hand woven wool, 48″×60″)

Rug
Nowetah Timmerman (Susquehanna-Cherokee), 1990
(hand woven wool, 32″×64″)

Madonna of Legends
Charles Vann (Cherokee), c 1980s
(charcoal on paper)

Charles Vann once asked his grandmother what women did when there was no one to assist them while they gave birth. She paused for a moment and said, 'When nature says its time, then that's what a woman will do. Women have been giving birth for thousands of years.' She went on to say she knew a lady who gave birth in a bare patch filled with vines and sticks. 'Sequoya was born this way. The Indian lives in the fields of life, so he begins at birth. The pain, discomfort and agony caused by birth is a small price for what is expected from every man.'

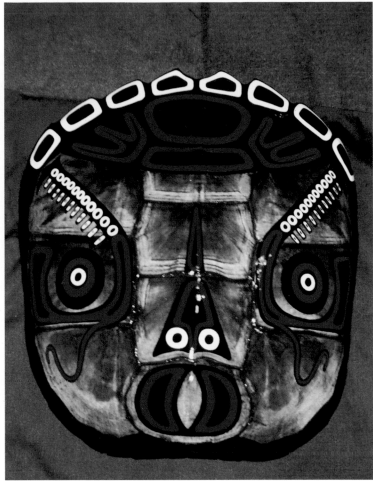

Shawl Dancer
Mary Adair (Cherokee), 1987

Turtle Shell Wall Hangings
Kevin Skypainter Turner (Choctaw), 1990
(enamel painted alligator snapping turtle shell)

A native of Oklahoma now living in Muskogee, Mary Adair studied art at Bacone College, Northeastern State University and Tulsa University, and earned her BA and ME degrees from NSU. She has been a professional artist since 1967. She has exhibited work in the Red Cloud Indian Art Show (Pine Ridge, SD), the Cherokee National Museum Art Show (Tahlequah, OK), the Five Civilized Tribes Museum Annual (Muskogee, OK), the Cherokee Museum (Cherokee, NC), Heard Museum (Phoenix, AZ) and the Philbrook Museum (Tulsa, OK). Her paintings can also be found in museums, libraries and private collections.

Her paintings usually depict Indian people doing everyday things or taking part in traditional ceremonies. She particularly enjoys painting children. Formerly the Executive Director of Murrow Indian Children's Home, she is currently also employed by the Cherokee Nation of Oklahoma.

HorseChief, her married name, was dropped from her signature when her son Samuel HorseChief and her daughter Mary Catherine HorseChief began painting professionally. Her father's family, Adair, is numerous among the Cherokee people, descending from the marriage of a Cherokee woman, Nancy Lightfoot, and an Irish-Scottish trader named Adair.

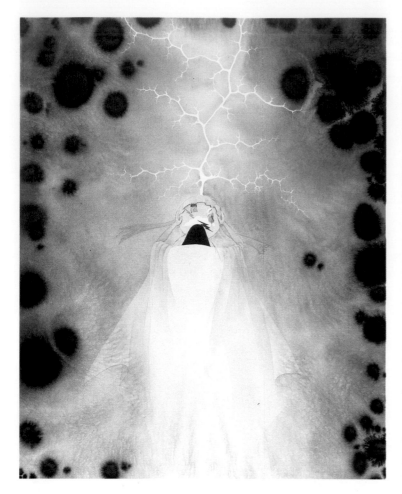

Protection and Direction
Connie Seabourn (Nged-Cherokee), 1991
(watercolor, 22″×15″)

The Sweetness of Your Touch
Connie Seabourn (Nged-Cherokee), 1991
(watercolor, 22″×15″)

Awakening
Connie Seabourn (Nged-Cherokee), 1991
(watercolor, 22″×15″)

Connie Seabourn dates her professional life as an artist from the time she entered the annual competition at the Five Civilized Tribes Museum (Muskogee, OK) in 1969. Her works were featured in nearly 20 solo shows and two dozen two-artist shows, and have been included in corporate and museum collections across the United States. In addition to translucent watercolor on paper, she works in opaque media on canvas and uses methods of multiple-originals, such as serigraphy and etching. She sees her work as a reflection of her culture, of 'listening, hearing and seeing.'

Pecan Picking Time
Joan Hill
(Creek tribal member with Cherokee ancestry), 1991
(watercolor-gouache, 7.5″×9.5″)

Originally grown in the lowlands of the Mississippi River basin, pecans were brought over the Trail of Tears when the Five Civilized Tribes were removed to Indian Territory. Redbird Harris, Hill's great-grandfather, carried pecans with him when he went to the 'new land in the West' (Oklahoma). This watercolor was the winner of the 1991 Masters Heritage Award at the Five Civilized Tribes Museum.

Baptism on the Trail
Joan Hill
(Creek tribal member with Cherokee ancestry), 1991
(watercolor-gouache, 21.5″×29.5″)

During the Trail of Tears period (1838-1839), strongly religious Cherokee groups, led by the Baptist ministers Jesse Bushyhead and Evan Jones, made an agreement with authorities that allowed them to rest on Sundays and conduct their accustomed religious services on the trail. The survival rates of these groups were much higher than any other group of immigrants on the Trail of Tears. The baptism depicted here is derived from verbal descriptions.

Sacred Ceremony of the Temple Mound
Joan Hill
(Creek tribal member with Cherokee ancestry), 1989
(acrylic on canvas, 32″ × 36″)

In the first Burial Mound Period in Native American prehistory, which lasted from 500 AD to 1300 AD, temples were built atop great, flat-topped earth mounds. The Temple Mound Period reached its peak between 1550 and 1650, marking the highest development achieved by Native Americans north of Mexico, and flourished in the rich agricultural lands of the Southeast. These ancient peoples are thought to be ancestors of the Five Civilized Tribes, in particular, the tribes of the Muskogean Confederacy. In Hill's painting, the chief, dressed in ceremonial clothing, greets his elder brother, the Sun, and shows him his course across the heavens.

Women's Voices at the Council
Joan Hill
(Creek tribal member with Cherokee ancestry), 1990
(acrylic on canvas, 28″ × 38″)

This painting depicts the importance of women in ancient Native American society. The painting's central focus is the Beloved Woman, who was head of her tribe's women's council and spoke for the Great Spirit. Because many Native American cultures were traditionally matriarchal, women were afforded great respect, having a voice in the daily affairs of their tribes or villages, and often casting the deciding votes for chieftainship. Commissioned by Governor Bellmon's Commission on the Status of Women to celebrate the Conference of Oklahoma Women, this painting is from the collection of the State of Oklahoma.

Medicine Wheel
Doug Coffin (Patawatomi)

   Doug Coffin is one of the great contemporary Native American artists. His work is collected by many museums and famous people including artist RC Gorman. Doug's work is shown at the Copeland Rutherford Fine Arts Gallery, Santa Fe, NM.

Untitled
Doug Coffin (Patawatomi)
(Contemporary totem)

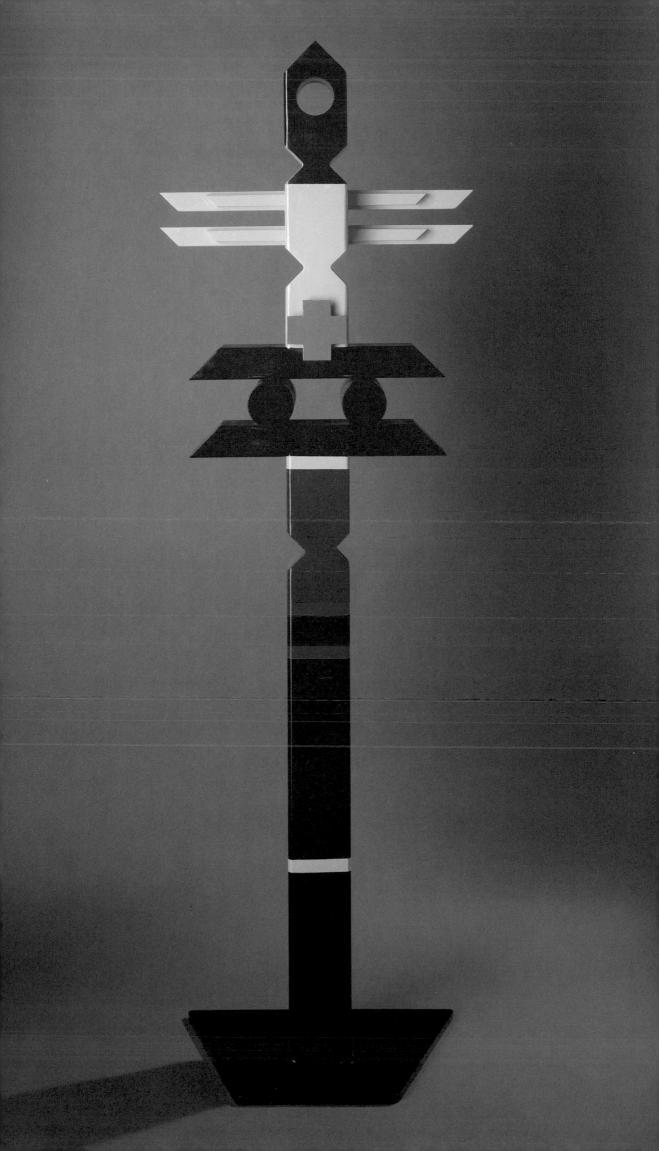

THE ART AND FOLKLORE

Above: In this photograph dating from the 1890s, a Hopi woman is shown dressing the hair of an unmarried girl. After a four-day ceremony of grinding corn in a dark room, a young girl proved that she was skilled at household chores. The ritual concluded with an older woman preparing the intricate squash blossom hairstyle that was the sign of her marriageable status. The process required great skill and could take over an hour to finish. The hair was parted into two sections, and each section was wrapped around a U-shaped bow in a complex bun arrangement. After marriage, young women braided their hair.

In terms of art and architecture, the cultures of the Southwest were among the most complex in prehistoric North America. Of all the areas north of Mexico, it is here that pre-Columbian architecture is most widely evident. Preserved for posterity by the dry air of the high desert are the remains of the settlements of the Anasazi people. They built cities with multistory apartment houses, such as the ones extant at Canyon de Chelly, AZ, and Chaco Canyon, NM, developed farming and flourished peacefully between roughly 700 AD and 1100 AD. Their culture was evidently based on a delicate climatic balance, which apparently collapsed in a period of severe droughts and/or natural disasters that occurred prior to 1350, by which time the Anasazi had disappeared and their place had been taken by the Zuni, Hopi, Navajo and Pueblo who inhabit this land today.

The Zuni and Hopi tribes, as well as the Pueblo, traditionally lived in adobe cities similar to those of the Anasazi, while the Navajo and Apache tribes traditionally lived a more nomadic life in the central and southern parts of Arizona and New Mexico, extending into part of Texas and northern Mexico. The Hopi, who dwell upon four mesas in northeastern Arizona, have been in place for about as long as any extant tribe in the United States. Farmers for centuries, they raise corn, beans, squash and tobacco on family plots that surround the pueblos. Like other pueblo-dwelling people, they also hunt rabbits and deer for meat and skins with which to make clothing.

One of the most intriguing aspects of Southwest ritual life and pictorial art is the Kachinas, spirits associated with initiation ceremonies of children at the age of ten. The Kachina ceremonial cycle begins at the Winter Solstice in midwinter with the annual opening of the Kiva–a subterranean chamber symbolizing the entrance to the underworld–and progresses through the false spring, or Powamu (bean dance) ritual in February. Dances associated with these festivals and rituals feature men wearing paint and costumes that represent specific Kachinas. In July, after the Summer Solice, the Kachina season ends when the Kachinas go back into the underworld.

Kachinas have been represented historically not only by the dancers but by dolls, which are miniatures of the Kachina dancers, and are presented ceremonially to infants of both

OF THE SOUTHWEST TRIBES

sexes and females of all ages. Traditionally considered sacred ritual objects–not toys–by Native Americans, early Christian missionaries considered the dolls demonic and vulgar. In the twentieth century, Kachinas became a valued collector's item for whites, and since the 1940s, many have been made specifically for the art market.

Kachina dolls are usually carved from the dried roots of cottonwood trees, as other native woods are considered inferior. The porous wood is primed with clay before painting. Paints are derived from mineral and vegetable pigments, and the colors represent the six cardinal directions: north (yellow), south (red), east (white), west (turquoise), up (black) and down (gray). Cloth, fur, leather and wooden parts are also

Below: Masked Koyemsi Kachinas (Mudheads) prepare to dance at the Zuni Pueblo in New Mexico in 1879, while spectators line the upper walls. All Zuni male youths were initiated into the Kachina Societies, and during dances they wore masks to impersonate Kachinas. Mudheads were clowns whose role was to entertain the audience. It was perhaps because of their nonserious, comedic nature that they were allowed to be photographed by white ethnographers.

Above: Southwest pottery motifs. The top two rows are Mimbres designs. The remainder are *(clockwise from top left):* Pima, Hopi, San Ildefonso Pueblo and Zuni.

Far Right: A late nineteenth century Navajo silversmith displays his work and his tools. The Navajos learned this trade from the Mexicans and created works of great beauty with primitive tools. Early jewelry was made from American or Mexican silver currency, until sheets of metal became available. The conchas shown here were used as hairpieces and also as belts.

attached. The feathers used in traditional Kachina dolls were from falcons, hawks and crows, and the down of eagles and owls was once highly prized. Since 1945, commercial Kachinas are known to include chicken feathers.

Kachina dolls represent dozens of specific Kachinas, and the mythology of most is still known.

The Navajo adulthood initiation was important in the overall cycle of tribal festivities, but not nearly as ornate as the Hopi Kachina ceremonies. The onset of puberty in girls was treated with a good deal less of the arms-length seen in other tribes in North America.

After elaborate coming-of-age rites, marriage among the tribes of the Southwest was anticlimactic. In fact, among the Navajos, a man could seal a nuptial pact by bringing a horse to give the family of his intended.

The Apaches comprised a series of subtribes spread across the entire southwestern desert, from Arizona to Texas and south into Mexico. They had no organized civic structure, and like the Athapaskans of the far north, their leadership came not from a carefully designated chief, but from the leader of an individual band who exhibited outstanding leadership traits. After this Athapaskan tribe migrated to the Southwest, it retained the hunting and foraging lifestyle of its ancestors.

The cultures of the Southwest peoples have remained the same for centuries. The visual arts have not only survived the encroachment of European-American culture, they have flourished. The pueblos are still thriving towns, the oldest continuously inhabited dwellings in North America. Motor vehicles and electricity have been added, but otherwise, life is surprisingly similar to what it must have been like centuries ago.

In the New Mexico town of Taos, which has grown up near Taos Pueblo, is an art market that is touted as being one of the four largest in the world, surpassed only by Paris, New York and neighboring Santa Fe. Much of the art marketed here features traditional Indian motifs and is created by Native American artists.

Traditionally, Southwestern art is dominated by abstract geometric designs, especially those woven into baskets and painted on pottery.

The sand paintings characteristic of this region employ conventional symbols for natural phenomena, such as the Sun, clouds and lightning.

The most naturalistic expression appears in the murals on the inside walls of religious structures and in ceremonial costumes that have their masks which depict anthropromorphic spirits.

Notable places in the Southwest where artifacts of the ancient native art and culture of the region may be viewed today include: Canyon de Chelly National Monument (AZ), Navajo National Monument (AZ), the Heard Museum (Phoenix, AZ), Mesa Verde National Park (CO), Chaco Culture National Historical Park (NM), and the Museum of Indian Arts and Culture (Santa Fe, NM).

Several pueblos, continuously inhabited for several centuries, are also open to the public. These include the Acoma, the Salinas, the Taos and the Zuni in New Mexico, and the Three Kiva Pueblo in Utah. The Homolovi Pueblo in Arizona is open but uninhabited.

Contemporary Native American Southwest art can be viewed at galleries throughout the region, such as the Museum of Northern Arizona (Flagstaff), the Indian Pueblo Cultural Center (Albuquerque, NM) and the Institute of American Indian Arts (Santa Fe, NM). The two latter institutions also host demonstrations and seasonal Native American festivals.

THE BEGINNING OF NEWNESS (A Zuni Legend)

Before the beginning of the New-making, the All-father Father alone had being. Through the ages, there was nothing else except black darkness. In the beginning of the New-making, the All-father Father thought outward in space, and mists were created and up-lifted. Thus through his knowledge he made himself the Sun, who was thus created and is the great Father. The dark spaces brightened with light. The cloud mists thickened and became water.

From his flesh, the Sun-father created the Seed-stuff of worlds, and he himself rested upon the waters. And these two—the Four-fold-containing Earth-mother and the All-covering Sky-father, the surpassing beings, with power of changing their forms even as smoke changes in the wind–were the father and mother of the soul-beings.

Then as man and woman spoke these two together. 'Behold!' said Earth-mother, as a great terraced bowl appeared at hand, and within it water. 'This shall be the home of my tiny children. On the rim of each world-country in which they wander, terraced mountains shall stand, making in one region

Above: Paliwahtiwa, the Zuni Governor in the late 1880s, wears the elaborate silver and turquoise jewelry commonly found among the tribes of the Southwest. The beaded crescent necklace resembles those of the Navajo.

many mountains by which one country shall be known from another.'

Then she spat on the water and struck it and stirred it with her fingers. Foam gathered about the terraced rim, mounting higher and higher. Then with her warm breath she blew across the terraces. White flecks of foam broke away and floated over the water. But the cold breath of Sky-father shattered the foam and it fell downward in fine mist and spray.

Then Earth-mother spoke. 'Even so shall white clouds float up from the great waters at the borders of the world, and clustering about the mountain terraces of the horizon, shall be broken and hardened by thy cold. Then will they shed downward, in rain-spray, the water of life, even into the hollow places of my lap. For in my lap shall nestle our children, mankind and creature-kind, for warmth in thy coldness.'

So even the trees on high mountains near the clouds and Sky-father, crouch low toward Earth-mother for warmth and protection. Warm is Earth-mother, cold our Sky-father.

Then Sky-father said, 'Even so. Yet I, too, will be helpful to our children.' Then he spread his hand out with the palm downward, and into all the wrinkles of this hand he set the semblance of shining yellow corn-grains. In the dark of the early world-dawn, they gleamed like sparks of fire.

'See,' he said, pointing to the seven grains between his thumb and four fingers, 'our children shall be guided by these when the Sun-father is not near and thy terraces are as darkness itself. Then shall our children by guided by lights.'

So Sky-father created the stars. Then he said, 'And even as these grains gleam up from the water, so shall seed grain like them spring up from the Earth when touched by water, to nourish our children.' And thus they created the seed-corn. And in many other ways they devised for their children, the soul-beings.

But the first children, in a cave of the Earth, were unfinished. The cave was of sooty blackness, black as a chimney at night-time, and foul. Loud became their murmurings and lamentations, until many sought to escape, growing wiser and more man-like.

But the Earth was not then as we now see it. Then the Sun-father sent down two sons (sons also of the Foam-cap), the Beloved Twain, Twin Brothers of Light, yet Elder and Younger, the right and the left, like to question and answer in deciding and doing. To them, the Sun-father imparted his own wisdom. He gave them the great cloud-bow, and for arrows the thunderbolts of the four quarters. For buckler, they had the fog-making shelf, spun and woven of the floating clouds and spray. The shield supports its bearer, as clouds are supported by the wind, yet hides its bearer also. And he gave to them the fathership and control of men and of all creatures. Then the Beloved Twain, with their great cloud-bow, lifted the Sky-father into the vault of the skies, that the Earth might become warm and fitter for men and creatures. Then along the Sun-seeking trail, they sped to the mountains westward. With magic knives they spread open the depths of the mountain and uncovered the cave in which dwelt the unfinished men and creatures. So they dwelt with men, learning to know them and seeking to lead them out.

Now there were growing things in the depths, like grasses and vines. So the Beloved Twain breathed on the stems, growing tall toward the light as grass is wont to do, making them stronger and twisting them upward until they formed a great ladder by which men and creatures ascended to a second cave.

Up the ladder into the second cave-world men and the beings crowded, following closely the Two Little but Mighty

Ones. Yet many fell back and were lost in the darkness. They peopled the underworld, from which they escaped after time, amid terrible Earth shakings.

In this second cave, it was as dark as the night of a stormy season, but larger of space and higher. Here again men and the beings increased, and their complainings grew loud. So the Twain again increased the growth of the ladder, and again led men upward, not all at once, but in six bands, to become the fathers of six kinds of men–the yellow, the tawny gray, the red, the white, the black and the mingled. And this time also many were lost or left behind.

Now the third great cave was larger and lighter, like a valley in starlight. And again they increased in number. And again the Two led them out into a fourth cave. Here it was light like dawning, and men began to perceive and to learn variously, according to their natures, wherefore the Twain taught them first to seek the Sun-father.

Then as the last cave became filled and men learned to understand, the Two led them forth again into the great upper world, which is the World of Knowing and Seeing.

When it rains, some Indian, sick in heaven, is weeping. Long, long ago, there was a good young Indian on Earth. When he died, the Indians wept so that a flood came upon the Earth and drowned all people except one couple.

THE CREATION OF THE WORLD (A Pima Legend)

In the beginning there was nothing at all except darkness. All was darkness and emptiness. For a long, long while, the darkness gathered until it became a great mass. Over this, the spirit of Earth Doctor drifted to and fro like a fluffy bit of cotton in the breeze.

Then Earth Doctor decided to make for himself an abiding place. So he thought within himself, 'Come forth, some kind of plant,' and there appeared the creosote bush. He placed this before him and set it upright. But it at once fell over. He set it upright again; again it fell. So it fell until the fourth time it remained upright. Then Earth Doctor took from his breast a little dust and flattened it into a cake. When the dust cake was still, he danced upon it, singing a magic song.

Next he created some black insects, which made black gum on the creosote bush. Then he made a termite, which worked with the small earth cake until it grew very large. As he sang and danced upon it, the flat world stretched out on all sides until it was as large as it is now. Then he made a round sky-cover to fit over it, round like the houses of the Pimas. But the Earth shook and stretched, so that it was unsafe. So Earth Doctor made a gray spider, which was to spin a web around the edges of the Earth and sky, fastening them together. When this was done, the Earth grew firm and solid.

Earth Doctor made water, mountains, trees, grass and weeds–made everything as we see it now. But all was still inky blackness. Then he made a dish, poured water into it, and it became ice. He threw this round block of ice far to the north, and it fell at the place where the Earth and sky were woven together. At once, the ice began to gleam and shine. We call it now the Sun. It rose from the ground in the north up into the sky and then fell back. Earth Doctor took it and threw it to the west where the Earth and sky were sewn together. It rose into the sky and again slid back to the Earth. Then he threw it to the far south, but it slid back again to the flat Earth.

At last he threw it to the east. It rose higher and higher in the sky until it reached the highest point in the round blue cover and began to slide down on the other side. And so the Sun does even yet.

Then Earth Doctor poured more water into the dish, and it became ice. He sang a magic song and threw the round ball of ice to the north where the Earth and sky are woven together. It gleamed and shone, but not so brightly as the Sun. It became the Moon, and it rose in the sky, but fell back again, just as the Sun had done. So he threw the ball to the west, and then to the south, but it slid back each time to the Earth. Then he threw it to the east, and it rose to the highest point in the sky-cover and began to slide down on the other side. And so it does even today, following the Sun.

But Earth Doctor saw that when the Sun and Moon were not in the sky all was inky darkness. So he sang a magic song and took some water into his mouth and blew it into the sky in a spray to make little stars. Then he took his magic crystal and broke it into pieces and threw them into the sky to make larger stars. Next he took his walking stick and placed ashes on the end of it. Then he drew it across the sky to form the Milky Way. So Earth Doctor made all the stars.

THE CREATION OF MANKIND AND THE FLOOD (A Pima Legend)

After the world had been created, Earth Doctor made many kinds of animals and creeping things. Then he made images of clay and told them to be people. After awhile, there were so many people that there was not enough food and water for all. They were never sick and none died. At last, there grew to be so many, they were obliged to eat each other. Then Earth Doctor, because he could not give them enough water and food, killed them all. He caught the hook of his staff into the sky and pulled it down so that it crushed all the people and all the animals, until there was nothing living on the Earth.

Earth Doctor made a hole through the Earth with his stick and through that he went, coming out safe, but alone, on the other side. He called upon the Sun and Moon to come out of the wreck of the world and sky, and they did so. But there was no sky for them to travel through, no stars and no Milky Way. So Earth Doctor made these all over again. Then he created another race of men and animals.

Then Coyote was born. Moon was his mother. When Coyote was large and strong, he came to the land where the Pima Indians lived. Next, Elder Brother was born. Earth was his mother and Sky his father. He was so powerful that he spoke roughly to Earth Doctor, who trembled before him. The people began to increase in numbers, just as they had done before, but Elder Brother shortened their lives, so the Earth did not become so crowded.

But Elder Brother did not like the people created by Earth Doctor, so he planned to destroy them again. So Elder Brother planned to create a magic baby.

The screams of the baby shook the Earth. They could be heard for a great distance. Then Earth Doctor called all the people together and told them there would be a great flood. He sang a magic song and then bored a hole through the flat earth-plain through to the other side. Some of the people went into the hole to escape the flood that was coming, but not very many got through. Some of the people asked Elder Brother to help them, but he did not answer. Only Coyote answered. He told Coyote to find a big log and sit on it, so that he would float on the surface of the water with the driftwood. Elder Brother got into a big olla, which he had made, and closed it tight. So he rolled along on the ground under the olla. He sang a magic song as he climbed into his olla.

A young man went to the place where the baby was screaming. Its tears were a great torrent which cut gorges in the Earth before it. The water was rising all over the Earth. He bent over the child to pick it up, and immediately both became birds and flew above the flood. Only five birds were saved from the flood. One was a flicker and one a vulture. They clung by their beaks to the sky to keep themselves above the waters, but the tail of the flicker was washed by the waves and that is why it is stiff to this day. At last, a god took pity on them and gave them power to make 'nests of down' from their own breasts on which they floated on the water. One of these birds was the vipisimal, and if anyone injures it to this day, the flood may come again.

South Doctor called his people to him and told them that a flood was coming. He sang a magic song, and he bored a hole in the ground with a cane so that people might go through to the other side. Others he sent to Earth Doctor, but Earth Doctor told them they were too late, so they sent the people to the top of a high mountain called Crooked Mountain. South Doctor sang a magic song and traced his cane around the mountain, but that held back the waters only for a short time. Four times he sang and traced a line around the mountain, yet the flood rose each time. There was only one thing more to do.

He held his magic crystals in his left hand and sang a song. Then he struck it with his cane. A thunder peal rang through the mountains. He threw his staff into the water, and it cracked with a loud noise.

Turning, he saw a dog near him. He said, 'How high is the tide?'

The dog said, 'It is very near the top.' He looked at the people as he said it.

When they heard the dog's voice, they all turned to stone. They stood just as they were, and they are there to this day in groups: some of the men talking, some of the women cooking and some crying.

But Earth Doctor escaped by enclosing himself in his reed staff, which floated upon the water. South Doctor rolled along in his olla until he came near the mouth of the Colorado River. The olla is now called Black Mountain. After the flood, he came out and visited all parts of the land. When he met Coyote and Earth Doctor, each claimed to have been the first to appear after the flood, but at last they admitted South Doctor was the first, so he became ruler of the world.

SPIDER'S CREATION (A Zia Legend)

In the beginning, long, long ago, there was but one being in the lower world. This was the spider, Sussistinnako. At that time, there were no other insects, no birds, animals or any other living creatures. The spider drew a line of meal from north to south and then crossed it with another line running east and west. On each side of the first line, north of the second, he placed two small parcels. They were precious, but no one knew what was in them except Spider. Then he sat down near the parcels and began to sing. The music was low and sweet, and the two parcels accompanied him, by shaking like rattles. Then two women appeared, one from each parcel.

In a short time, people appeared and began walking around. Then animals, birds and insects appeared, and Spider continued to sing until his creation was complete.

But there was no light, and as there were many people, they did not pass about much for fear of treading upon each other.

The two women first created were mothers of all. One was named Utset, and she was the mother of all Indians. The other was Now-utset, and she was the mother of all other nations. While it was still dark, Spider divided the people into clans, saying to some, 'You are of the Corn clan, and you are the first of all.' To others he said, 'You belong to the Coyote clan.' So he divided them into their clans, the clans of the Bear, the Eagle and other clans.

After Spider had nearly created the Earth, Ha-arts, he thought it would be well to have rain to water it, so he created the Cloud People, the Lightning People, the Thunder People and the Rainbow People to work for the people of Ha-arts, the Earth. He divided this creation into six parts, and each had its home in a spring in the heart of a great mountain upon whose summit was a giant tree. One was in the spruce tree on the Mountain of the North; another in the pine tree on the Mountain of the West; another in the oak tree on the Mountain of the South; and anotherin the aspen tree on the Mountain of the East; the fifth was on the cedar tree on the Mountain of Zenith; and the last in an oak tree on the Mountain of the Nadir.

Spider divided the world into three parts: Ha-arts, the Earth, Tinia, the middle plain and Hu-wa-ka, the upper plain. Then Spider gave to these People of the Clouds and to the rainbow, Tinia, the middle plain.

Now it was still dark, but the people of Ha-arts made houses for themselves by digging in the rocks and the Earth. They could not build houses as they do now, because they could not see.

In a short time, Utset and Now-utset talked much to each other, saying, 'We will make light, that our people may see. We cannot tell the people now, but tomorrow will be a good day and the day after tomorrow will be a good day,' meaning that their thoughts were good. So they spoke with one tongue. They said 'Now all is covered with darkness, but after awhile we will have light.'

Then these two mothers, being inspired by Sussistinnako, the spider, made the Sun from white shell, turkis, red stone and abalone shell. After making the Sun, they carried him to the east and camped there, since there were no houses. The next morning, they climbed to the top of a high mountain and dropped the Sun down behind it. After a time, he began to ascend. When the people saw the light, they were happy.

When the Sun was far off, his face was blue; as he came nearer, his face grew brighter. Yet they did not see the Sun himself, but only a large mask which covered his whole body.

The people saw that the world was large and the country beautiful. When the two mothers returned to the village, they said to the people, 'We are the mothers of all.'

The Sun lighted the world during the day, but there was no light at night. So the two mothers created the Moon from a slightly black stone, many kinds of yellow stone, turkis and a red stone, that the world might be light at night. But the Moon traveled slowly and did not always give light. Then the two mothers created the Star People and made their eyes of sparkling white crystal, that they might twinkle and brighten the world at night. When the Star People lived in the lower world, they were gathered into beautiful groups. They were not scattered about as they are in the upper world.

THE GREAT FLOOD
(A Zia Legend)

For a long time after the fight, the people were very happy, but the ninth year was very bad. The whole Earth was filled with water. The water did not fall in rain, but came in as rivers between the mesas. It continued to flow in from all sides until the people and the animals fled to the mesa tops. The water continued to rise until nearly level with the tops of the mesas.

Then Sussistinnako cried, 'Where shall my people go? Where is the road to the north?' He looked to the north. 'Where is the road to the west? Where is the road to the east? Where is the road to the south?' He looked in each direction. He said, 'I see the waters are everywhere.'

All of the medicine men sang four days and four nights, but still the waters continued to rise.

Spider placed a huge reed upon the top of the mesa. He said, 'My people will pass up through this to the world above.'

Utset led the way, carrying a sack in which were many of the Star People. The medicine men followed, carrying sacred things in sacred blankets on their backs. Then came the people and the animals and the snakes and birds. The turkey was far behind, and the foam of the water rose and reached the top

ends of his feathers. You may know that is true, because, even to this day, they bear the mark of the waters.

When they reached the top of the great reed, the Earth, which formed the floor of the world above, barred their way. Utset called to Locust, 'Man, come here.' Locust went to her. She said, 'You know best how to pass through the Earth. Go and make a door for us.'

'Very well, mother,' said Locust. 'I think I can make a way.'

He began working with his feet, and after a while, he passed through the earthy floor, entering the upper world. As soon as he saw it, he said to Utset, 'It is good above.'

Utset called Badger and said, 'Make a door for us. Sika, the Locust has made one, but it is very small.'

'Very well, mother, I will,' said Badger.

After much work, he passed into the world above and said, 'Mother, I have opened the way.' Badger also said, 'Father-mother, the world above is good.'

Utset then called Deer. She said, 'You go through first. If you can get your head through, others may pass.'

The deer returned saying, 'Father, it is all right. I passed without trouble.'

Utset called Elk. She said, 'You pass through. If you can get your head and horns through the door, all may pass.'

Elk returned saying, 'Father it is good. I passed without trouble.'

Then Utset told Buffalo to try, and he returned saying,

'Father-mother, the door is good. I passed without trouble.'

Utset called Scarab Beetle and gave him the sack of stars, telling him to pass out first with them. Scarab did not know what the sack contained, but he was very small and grew tired carrying it. He wondered what could be in the sack. After entering the new world, he was so tired he laid down the sack and peeped into it. He cut only a tiny hole, but at once the Star People flew out and filled the heavens everywhere.

Utset and all the people came, and after Turkey passed, the door was closed with a great rock so that the waters from below could not follow them.

Utset looked for the sack with the Star People. She found it nearly empty and could not tell where the stars had gone. The little beetle sat by, very much frightened and very sad. But Utset was angry and said, 'You are bad and disobedient. From this time forth, you shall be blind.' That is the reason the scrabaeus has no eyes, so the old ones say.

But the little fellow had saved a few of the stars by grasping the sack and holding it fast. Utset placed these in the heavens. In one group she placed seven–the great bear. In another, three. In another group she placed the Pleiades, and threw the others far off into the sky.

THE CORN MAIDENS
(A Zuni Legend)

After long ages of wandering, the precious Seed-things rested over the Middle at Zuni, and men turned their hearts to the cherishing of their corn and the Corn Maidens instead of warring with strange men. But there was complaint by the people of the customs followed. Some said the music was not that of the olden time. Far better was that which of nights they often heard as they wandered up and down the river trail. Wonderful music, as of liquid voices in caverns, or the echo of women's laughter in water-vases. And the music was timed with a deep-toned drum from the Mountain of Thunder. Others thought the music was that of the ghosts of ancient men, but it was far more beautiful than the music when danced the Corn Maidens. Others said light clouds rolled upward from the grotto in Thunder Mountain like the mists that leave behind them the dew. But lo! even as they faded, the bright garments of the Rainbow women might be seen fluttering, and the embroidery and paintings of these dances of the mist were more beautiful than the costumes of the Corn Maidens.

The priest of the people said, 'It may well be Paiyatuma, the liquid voices of his flute and the flutes of his players.'

When the time of ripening corn was near, the fathers ordered preparation for the dance of the Corn Maidens. They sent the two Master-Priests of the Bow to the grotto at Thunder Mountain saying, 'If you behold Paiyatuma and his maidens, perhaps they will give us the help of their customs.'

Up the river trail, the priests heard the sound of a drum and strains of song. It was Paiyatuma and his seven maidens, the Maidens of the House of Stars, sisters of the Corn Maidens.

The God of Dawn and Music lifted his flute and took his place in the line of dancers. The drum sounded until the cavern shook as with thunder. The flutes sang and sighed as the wind in a wooded canyon while still the storm is distant. White mists floated up from the wands of the Maidens, above which fluttered the butterflies of Summer-land about the dress of the Rainbows in the strange, blue light of the night.

Paiyatuma, smiling, said, 'Go the way before, telling the fathers of our custom, and straight-away we will follow.'

Soon the sound of music was heard, coming from up the river, and soon the Flute People and singers and maidens of the flute dance. Up rose the fathers and all the watching people, greeting the God of Dawn with outstretched hands and offerings of prayer meal. The singers took their places and sounded their drums, flutes and song of clear waters, while the Maidens of the Dew danced their Flute dance. Greatly marveled the people, when from the wands they bore came forth white clouds, and fine, cool mists descended.

When the dance was ended and the Dew Maidens had retired, out came the beautiful Mothers of Corn. And when the players of the flutes saw them, they were enamored of their beauty and gazed upon them so intently that the Maidens let fall their hair and cast down their eyes. Jealous and bolder grew the mortal youths, and in the morning dawn, in rivalry, the dancers sought all too freely the presence of the Corn Maidens, no longer holding them so precious as in the olden time. And the matrons, intent on the new dance, heeded naught else.

The mists increased greatly, surrounding dances and watchers alike, until within them, the Maidens of Corn, all in white garments, became invisible. Then, sadly and noiselessly, they stole in amongst the people and laid their corn wands down amongst the trays, and laid their white embroidered garments thereupon, as mothers lay soft quilting over their babes. As the mists became thicker and began to drift, they fled away to the far south Summer-land.

The people in their trouble called the two Master-Priests and said: 'Who, now, think you, should journey to seek our precious Maidens? Who amongst the Beings is even as you are, strong of will and good of eyes? There is our great elder brother and father, Eagle, he of the floating down and of the terraced tailfan. Surely he is enduring of will and surpassing of sight.'

'Yea. Most surely,' said the fathers. 'Go forth and beseech him.'

The two hurried north to Twin Mountain, where in a grotto high up among the crags, with his mate and his young, dwelt the Eagle of the White Bonnet.

They climbed the mountain, but behold! Only the eaglets were there. They screamed lustily and tried to hide themselves in the dark recesses. 'Pull not our feathers, you of hurtful touch, but wait. When we are older, we will drop them for you even from the clouds.'

'Hush,' said the warriors. 'Wait in peace. We seek not you but your father.'

Then from afar, with a frown, came old Eagle. 'Why disturb my featherlings?' he cried.

'Father and elder brother, we come seeking only the light of your favor. Listen!' Then they told him of the lost Maidens of the Corn and begged him to search for them.

"Be it well with your wishes," said Eagle. 'Go you before contentedly.'

The warriors returned to the council, but Eagle winged his way high into the sky. High, high, he rose, until he circled among the clouds, small-seeming and swift, like seed-down in a whirlwind. Through all the heights, to the north, to the west, to the south and to the east, he circled and sailed. Yet nowhere saw he any trace of the Corn Maidens. Then he flew lower, returning. Before the warriors were rested, people heard the roar of his wings. As he alighted, the fathers said, 'Enter though and sit, oh brother, and say to us what you have to say.' And they offered him a pipe.

When they had puffed the smoke toward the four points of the compass and Eagle had purified his breath with smoke and had blown smoke over sacred things, he spoke.

'Far have I journeyed, scanning all the regions. Neither Bluebird nor Woodrat can hide from my seeing,' he said, snapping his beak. 'Neither of them, unless they hide under bushes. Yet I have failed to see anything of the Maidens you seek for. Send for my younger brother, the Falcon. Strong of flight is he, yet not so strong as I, and nearer the ground he takes his way toward sunrise.'

The Eagle spread his wings and flew away to Twin Mountain. The Warrior-Priests of the Bow sped again fleetly over the plain to the westward for his younger brother, Falcon. The warriors found Falcon sitting on an anthill. he paused as they approached, crying, 'If ye have snare strings, I will be off like the flight of an arrow well plumed of our feathers!'

'No,' said the priest. 'Your brother has bid us to seek you.'

They told Falcon what had happened and how Eagle had failed to find the Corn Maidens, so white and beautiful.

'Failed!' said Falcon. 'Of course he failed. He climbs aloft to the clouds and thinks he can see under every bush and into every shadow, as sees the Sun-father who sees not with eyes. Go you before.'

Before the Warrior-Priests had turned toward the town, the Falcon had spread his sharp wings and was skimming off over the tops of the trees and bushes as though verily seeking for field mice or birds' nests. The warriors returned to tell the fathers and to await his coming.

After Falcon had searched over the world, to the north and west, to the east and south, he, too, returned and was received as had been Eagle. He settled on the edge of a tray before the altar, as on the ant hill he settles today. When he had smoked and had been smoked, as had been Eagle, he told the sorrowing fathers and mothers that he had looked behind every copse and cliff shadow, but of the Maidens he had found no trace.

'They are hidden more closely than ever Sparrow hid,' he said. Then he, too, flew away to his hills in the west.

'Our beautiful Maiden Mothers,' cried the matrons. 'Lost, lost as the dead are they!'

'Yes,' said the others. 'Where now shall we seek them? The far-seeing Eagle and the close-searching Falcon alike have failed to find them.'

'Stay now your feet with patience,' said the fathers. Some of them had heard Raven, who sought food in the refuse and dirt at the edge of town at daybreak.

'Look now,' they said. "There is Heavy-nose, whose beak never fails to find the substance of see itself, however little or well hidden it is. He surely must know of the Corn Maidens. Let us call him.'

So the warriors went to the river side. When they found Raven, they raised their hands, all weaponless. 'We carry no pricking quills,' they called. 'Black-banded father, we seek your aid. Look now! The Mother-maidens of Seed, whose substance is the food alike of thy people and our people, have fled away. Neither our grandfather the Eagle nor his younger brother the Falcon can trace them. We beg you to aid us or counsel us.'

'Ka Ka!' cried the Raven. 'Too hungry am I to go abroad fasting on business for you. You are stingy! Here have I been since perching time, trying to find a throatful, but you pick the bones and lick the bowls too clean for that, be sure.'

'Come in, then, poor grandfather. We will give thee food to eat. Yea, and a cigarette to smoke, with all the ceremony.'

'Say you so?' said the Raven. He ruffled his collar and opened his mouth so wide with a lusty kaw-la-ka that he might well have swallowed his own head. 'Go you before,' he said, and followed them into the court of the dancers.

He was not ill to look upon. Upon his shoulders were bands of white cotton, and his back was blue, gleaming like the hair of a maiden dancer in the sunlight. The Master-Priest greeted Raven, bidding him sit and smoke.

'Ha! There is corn in this, else why the stalk of it?' said the Raven when he took the cane cigarette of the far spaces and noticed the joint of it. Then he did as he had seen the Master-Priest do, only more greedily. He sucked in such a throatful of smoke, fire and all, that it almost strangled him. He coughed and grew giddy, and the smoke, all hot and stinging, went through every part of him. It filled all his feathers, making even his brown eyes bluer and blacker, in rings. It is not to be wondered at, the blueness of flesh, blackness of dress and skinniness, yes, and tearfulness of eye which we see in the Raven today. And they are all as greedy of corn food as ever, for behold! No sooner had the old Raven recovered than he espied one of the ears of corn half hidden under the mantle-covers of the trays. He leaped from his place, laughing. They always laugh when they find anything, these ravens. Then he caught up the ear of corn and made off with it over the heads of the people and the tops of the houses, crying, 'Ha! Ha! In this wise and in no other will you find thy Seed Maidens.'

After a while, he came back saying, 'A sharp eye have I for the flesh of the Maidens. But who might see their breathing-beings, you dolts, except by the help of the Father of Dawn-Mist himself, whose breath makes breath of others seem as itself.' Then he flew away cawing.

The elders said to each other, 'It is our fault, so how dare we prevail on our father Paiyatuma to aid us? He warned us of this in the old time.'

Suddenly, for the Sun was rising, they heard Paiyatuma in his daylight mood and transformation. Thoughtless and loud, uncouth in speech, he walked along the outskirts of the village. He joked fearlessly even of fearful things, for all his words and deeds were the reverse of his sacred being. He sat down on a heap of vile refuse, saying he would have a feast.

'My poor little children,' he said, as he spoke to aged priest and white-haired matrons. 'Good night to you all,' he said, though it was dawn. He perplexed them with his speeches.

'We beseech a favor, oh father, and your aid in finding our beautiful Maidens,' so the priests mourned.

"Oh, that is all is it? But why find that which is not lost, or summon those who will not come?"

Then he reproached them for not preparing the sacred plumes and picked up the very plumes he had said were not there.

The wise Pekwinna, the Speaker of the Sun, took two plumes and the banded wing-tips of the turkey, and, approaching Paiyatuma, stroked him with the tips of the feathers and then laid the feathers upon his lips.

Paiyatuma became aged and grand and straight, as a tall tree shorn by lightning. He said to the father: 'Thou are wise of thought and good of heart. Therefore, I will summon from Summer-land the beautiful Maidens that you may look upon them once more and make an offering of plumes in sacrifice for them, but they are lost as dwellers amongst you.'

He told them of the song lines and the sacred speeches and of the offering of the sacred plume wands, and then turned about and sped away so fleetly that none saw him.

Beyond the first valley of the high plain to the south, Paiyatuma planted the four plume wands. First he planted the yellow, bending over it and watching it. When it ceased to flutter, the soft down on it leaned northward but moved not. Then he set the blue wand and watched it; then the white wand. The eagle down on them leaned to right and left and still northward, yet moved not. Farther on, he planted the red wand, and, bending low, without breathing, watched it closely. The soft down plumes began to wave as though blown by the breath of some small creature. Backward and forward, northward and southward they swayed, as if in time to the breath of one resting.

'It is the breath of the Maidens in Summer-land, for the plumes of the southland sway soft to their gentle breathing. So shall it ever be. When I set the down of my mists on the plains and scatter my bright beads in the northland, summer shall go thither from afar, borne on the breath of the Seed Maidens. Where they breathe, warmth, showers and fertility shall follow with the birds of Summer-land and the butterflies, northward over the world.'

Paiyatuma arose and sped by the magic of his knowledge into the countries of Summer-land. He fled swiftly and silently as the soft breath he sought for, bearing his painted flute before him. When he paused to rest, he played on his painted flute, and the butterflies and birds sought him. So he sent them to seek the Maidens, following swiftly, and, long before he found them, he greeted them with the music of his song-sound, even as the People of the Seed now greet them in the song of the dancers.

When the Maidens heard his music and saw his tall form in their great fields of corn, they plucked ears, each of her own kind, and with them filled their colored trays and over all spread embroidered mantles–embroidered in all the bright colors and with the creature-songs of Summer-land, and so they sallied forth to meet him and welcome him.

He greeted them, each with the touch of his hands and the breath of his flute, and bade them follow him to the northland home of their deserted children.

By the magic of their knowledge they sped back as the stars speed over the world at nighttime, toward the home of our ancients. Only at night and dawn they journeyed, as the dead do, and the stars also. So they came at evening in the full of the last Moon to the Place of the Middle, bearing their trays of seed.

Glorious was Paiyatuma as he walked into the courts of the dancers in the dusk of the evening and stood with folded arms at the foot of the bow-fringed ladder of priestly counsel, he and his follower Shutsukya. He was tall and beautiful and banded with his own mists, and carried the banded wings of the turkeys with which he had winged his flight from afar, leading the

These Pages: Taos Pueblo, New Mexico. The word 'pueblo' comes from the Spanish word for 'village' or 'people' and is applied to the tribes who built cities out of sandstone and adobe in the arid regions of Arizona and New Mexico. Today, Taos is still inhabited by Pueblo Indians and is known as an artist colony where fine pottery, baskets, weaving and other traditional crafts are produced by skilled artisans.

Maidens, and followed as by his own shadow by the black being of the corn-soot, Shutsukya, who cries with the voice of the frost wind when the corn has grown aged and the harvest is taken away.

Surpassingly beautiful were the Maidens clothed in the white cotton and embroidered garments of Summer-land.

After long praying and chanting by the priests, the fathers of the people and those of the Sea and Water and the keepers of sacred things, the Maiden-mother of the north advanced to the foot of the ladder. She lifted from her head the beautiful tray of yellow corn and Paiyatuma took it. He pointed it to the regions, each in turn, and the Priest of the North came and received the tray of sacred seed.

Then the Maiden of the West advanced and gave up her tray of blue corn. Each in turn the Maidens gave up their trays of precious seed. The Maiden of the South, the red seed; the Maiden of the East, the white seed; then the Maiden with the black seed, and lastly, the tray of all-color seed, which the Priestess of Seed-and-All herself received.

The Maidens stood as before, she of the North at the northern end, but with her face southward looking far; she of the West, next, and lo! so all of them, with the seventh and last, looking southward. Standing thus, the darkness of the night fell around them. As shadows in deep night, so these Maidens of the Seed of Corn, the beloved and beautiful, were seen no more of men.

Paiyatuma stood alone, for Shutsukya walked now behind the Maidens, whistling shrilly, as the frost wind whistles when the corn is gathered away, among the lone canes and dry leaves of a gleaned field.

Below: Cottage industries are the mainstay of economic life on the Navajo Reservation in northwestern New Mexico. Outside the hogan, several Navajo women card the wool with modern equipment, but spin the yarn on old-style wooden spindles, twisting the wool into the required thickness. The Pueblos taught the Navajos the art of weaving. Novices quickly learned to create the high-quality, intricately designed blankets and rugs.

THE SONG-HUNTER
(A Navajo Legend)

A man sat thinking. 'Let me see. My songs are too short. I want more songs. Where shall I go to find them?'

Hasjelti appeared, and, perceiving his thoughts, said, 'I know here you can get more songs.'

'Well, I want to get more. So I will follow you.'

They went to a certain point in a box canyon in the Big Colorado River, and here they found four gods, the Host-jobokon, at work, hewing cottonwood logs.

Hasjelti said, 'This will not do. Cottonwood becomes water-soaked. You must use pine instead of cottonwood.'

The Hostjobokon began boring the pine with flint, but Hasjelti said, 'That is slow work.' He commanded a whirlwind to hollow the log. A cross, joining at the exact middle of each log, a solid one and the hollow one, was formed. The arms of the cross were equal.

The song-hunter entered the hollow log and Hasjelti closed the end with a cloud so that water would not enter when the logs were launched upon the great waters.

The logs floated off, and the Hostjobokon, accompanied by their wives, rode upon the logs, one couple sitting upon each arm. Hasjelti, Hostjoghon and the two Naaskiddi walked upon the banks to keep the logs offshore. Hasjelti carried a squirrel skin filled with tobacco, with which to supply the gods on their journey. Hostjoghon carried a staff ornamented with eagle and turkey plumes and a gaming ring with two hum-mingbirds tied to it with white cotton cord. The two Naaskiddi carried staffs of lightning. The Naaskiddi had clouds upon their backs in which the seeds of all corn and grasses were carried.

After floating a long distance down the river, they came to waters that had a shore on one side only. Here they landed. Here they found a people like themselves.

When these people learned of the Song-hunter, they gave him many songs and they painted pictures on a cotton blanket and said, 'These pictures must go with the songs. If we give this blanket to you, you will lose it. We will give you white earth and black coals which you will grind together to make black paint, and we will give you white sand, yellow sand and red sand. For the blue paint, you will take white sand and black coals with a very little red and yellow sand. These will give you blue.'

And so the Navajo people make blue, even to this day.

The Song-hunter remained with these people until the corn was ripe. There he learned to eat corn, and he carried some back with him to the Navajos, who had not seen corn before, and he taught them how to raise it and how to eat it.

When he wished to return home, the logs would not float upstream. Four sunbeams attached themselves to the logs, one to each cross arm, and so drew the Song-hunter back to the box canyon from which he had started.

When he reached that point, he separated the logs. He placed the end of the solid log into the hollow end of the other and planted this great pole in the river. It may be seen there today by the venturesome. In early days, many went there to pray and make offerings.

The Sand Painting of the Song-Hunter

The black cross bars denote pine logs, the white lines the froth of the water, the yellow, vegetable debris gathered by the logs, the blue and red lines, sunbeams. The blue spot in the center of the cross denotes water. There are four Hostjobokon, with their wives, the Hostjoboard.

Each couple sits upon one of the cross arms of the logs. The gods carry a rattle in their right hands, and in their left are springs of pinon. The goddesses carry pinon sprigs in both hands.

Hasjelti is at the east in the painting carrying a squirrel skin filled with tobacco. His shirt is white cotton and very elastic. The leggings are of white deerskin, fringed, and his head is ornamented with an eagle's tail. At the tip of each plume there is a fluffy feather from the breast of the eagle. The projection on the right of the throat is a fox skin.

Hostjoghon is at the west. His shirt is invisible, the dark being the dark of the body. His staff is colored black from a charred plant, and two strips of beaver skin tipped with six quills of the porcupine are attached to the right of the throat. The four colored stars on the body are bead ornaments. The top of the staff is ornamented with a turkey's tail. Eagle and turkey plumes are alternately attached to the staff.

The Naaskiddi are at the north and south of the painting carrying staffs of lightning ornamented with eagle plumes and sunbeams. Their bodies are nude except for loin skirts. The hunch upon the back is a black cloud, and the three groups of white lines indicate corn and other seeds. Five eagle plumes are attached to the cloud-back, since eagles live among the clouds. The body is surrounded by sunlight. The lines of blue and red which border the cloud-back denote sunbeams penetrating storm clouds. The black circle zig-zagged with white around the head is a cloud basket filled with corn and seeds of grass, and on each side of the head are five feathers of the red-shafted flicker.

The Rainbow goddess, upon which these gods often travel, partly encircles and completes the picture. These sand pictures are drawn upon common yellow sand, carried in blankets and laid in squares about three inches thick and four feet in diameter. The colors typically used in decoration are yellow, red and white, secured from sand stones, black from charcoal and a grayish-blue made from white sand and charcoal mixed with a very small quantity of yellow and red sands.

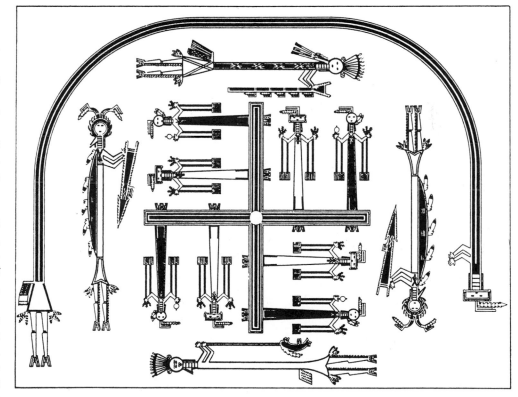

Pictograph showing People Wearing Jewelry
Anasazi, 700 to 1200 AD
(paint on rock)

Three painted figures on the canyon wall in Canyon-lands National Park. The dark red color comes from hematite, a dark red iron oxide mineral that is common to canyon country. The white, from gypsum, lime or chalk.

The White House
Anasazi, 1100 to 1200 AD
(cliff dwellings)

This apartment structure built in the sandstone cliffs at Canyon de Chelly, Arizona, once housed hundreds of Anasazi families. To the Navajos who came later, they were known as the 'Ancient Ones.'

Pictograph of a Human Figure
Anasazi, 800 BC to 1100 AD
(paint on rock)

A pictograph is made by applying organic or mineral pigment on rock with a finger or brush. It was a practice of many prehistoric people who settled in the Four Corners area of the United States, between Utah, Colorado, New Mexico and Arizona. The pictographs that have been discovered here are 800 to 1000 years old.

Pictograph Involving the Hands of the Artist
Anasazi, 800 BC to 1200 AD
(paint on rock)

These handprints are the work of prehistoric spray paint artists. Pigments were held in the mouth and blown over the hand leaving a negative image. It is impossible to determine the significance of the handprints. It could be the prints of the people who lived there or a warning rather than a welcome. Nonetheless, the handprints are a vivid reminder of the early cliff dwellers and their brief but fascinating history.

Pictograph involving Human Figures,
Animals and Other Symbols
Anasazi, 500 to 1200 AD

The bighorn sheep represented here are native to this
area of Canyonlands National Park.

Chapin Black-on-White Bowl
Anasazi, c 575-600 to 875-900 AD;
incidence decreases after 750 AD
(ceramic)

Chapin Gray Jar
Anasazi, c 575-900 AD
(ceramic)

Bluff Black-on-Red Bowl
Anasazi, c 750-900 AD
(ceramic)

Mesa Verde Black-on-White Jar
Anasazi, c 750-900 AD
(ceramic)

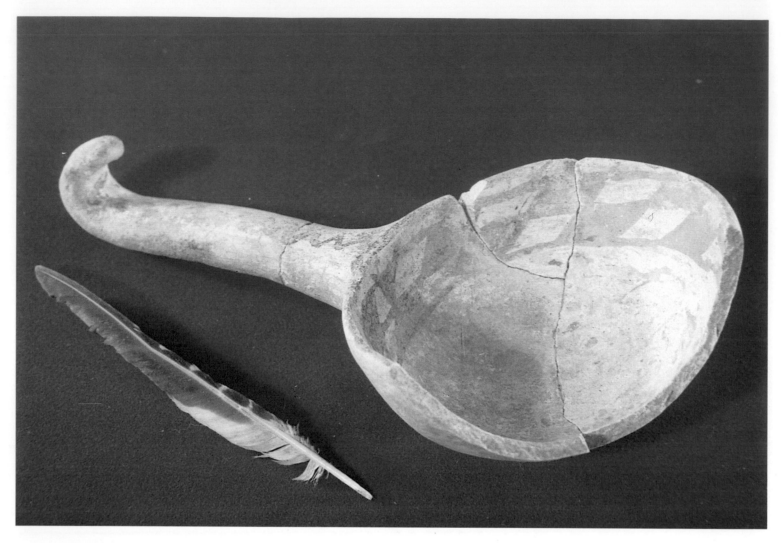

Cortez Black-on-White Ladle
Anasazi, c 900-1000 AD
(ceramic)

Mancos Black-on-White Duck Effigy
Anasazi, c 900-1150 AD
(ceramic)

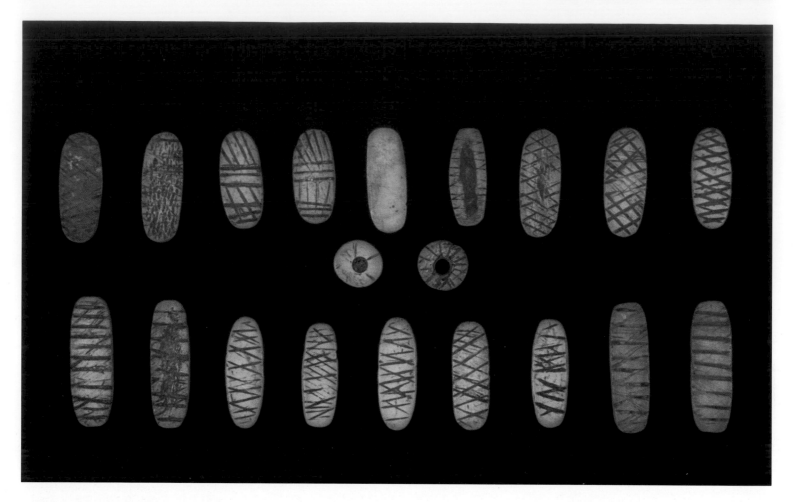

Circular Drilled and Tabular Gaming Pieces
Anasazi, 575-1000 AD
(stone)

Mancos Black-on-White Jar
Anasazi, c 900-1150 AD
(ceramic)

Mesa Verde Black-on-White Bowl
Anasazi, Pueblo III, c 1200-1300 AD
(ceramic)

Mesa Verde Corrugated Jar with Spiral Applique
Anasazi, c 1100-1300 AD
(ceramic)

Acoma Jar
Acoma Pueblo, early nineteenth century
(ceramic)

Water Jar
Zuni, c 1838
(ceramic)

Coiled Jar
Apache, nineteenth century
(woven reeds)

Coiled Bowl
Apache, nineteenth century
(woven reeds)

Cluster Squash Necklace (*Above Left*)
Zuni, 1920s
(Silver and turquoise;
beads from Fox or Cortez Mine, New Mexico)

Necklace (*Above Center*)
Zuni, 1920s
(Silver and turquoise;
beads from Cortez Mine, New Mexico)

Necklace (*Above Right*)
Fred Peshlaka (Navajo-Ya-ta-hey), 1920s
(Silver and turquoise;
beads from Blue Gem Mine, New Mexico)

Handled Water Jug
Navajo, nineteenth century
(ceramic)

Po-Okang-Hoya (Little War God) Kachina
Hopi, early twentieth century
(painted and carved cottonwood root)

Sotuknangu (God of the Sky) Kachina
Hopi, early twentieth century
(painted and carved cottonwood root)

Associated with the morning star, Sotuknangu is a warrior deity portrayed in Soyohim (mixed) dances by elders or clergy. Thought to control thunder and lightning, he carries the pantagraphic sticks, which represent the latter.

Masau'u (Earth God) Kachina
Hopi, early twentieth century
(painted and carved cottonwood root)

As Earth god, Masau'u controls the underworld as well as the surface, and as such, he also controls the passage of Kachinas between the living world and nether world via the Kiva.

Jemez/Hemis 'Flat Board' Kachina
Zuni, late nineteenth century
(painted and carved cottonwood root)

Associated with ripened corn, the Jemez or Hemis Kachina originated with the Zuni, but has been adopted by the Hopi as well.

Kweo (Wolf) Kachina
Hopi, early twentieth century
(painted and carved cottonwood root)

Characterized by large teeth and real fur, the wolf Kachina is a side dancer who accompanies the deer and ram Kachinas in Soyohim (mixed) dances. He holds a stick that represents the underbrush in which he hides while stalking his prey.

Patun (Squash) Kachina
Hopi, early twentieth century
(painted and carved cottonwood root)

The distinctive Patun Kachina (Wuya) of the Pumpkin Clan appears as a runner on First Mesa. Although the Patun Kachina is commonly seen, much of the mythology of the Pumpkin Clan has been lost. The yellow devices represent squash blossoms.

Mosairu (Buffalo?) Kachina
Hopi, early twentieth century
(painted and carved cottonwood root)

The horns, face and rattle suggest that this figure represent the Mosairu (buffalo) Kachina. It appears in the plaza dance along with other Soyohim (mixed) dancers. Recently depicted with black faces (seen here), Mosairu Kachinas were originally painted with turquoise faces.

Honan (Badger) Kachina
Hopi, early twentieth century
(painted and carved cottonwood root)

The Honan Kachina in Hopi culture is a curing Kachina identified by the badger tracks on its cheeks. It is also characterized by the feather arrangement on the headdress. The example pictured is possibly of the Second Mesa type found during February at the Powamu (bean dance or false spring) and Pachavu (tribal initiation) ceremonies.

Soyoko Mana (Ogre Woman) Kachina
Hopi, early twentieth century
(painted and carved cottonwood root)

The Soyoko Mana and the related Soyok'Wuhti appear during the Powamu Ceremony in February de-
manding food and/or threatening to eat children who
do not become slaves.

Soyoko-Mana (Ogre Woman) Kachina
Hopi, early twentieth century
(painted and carved cottonwood root)

The Soyoko Mana is characterized by long, stringy
hair and arms that are blood-stained from brutally catching, slaughtering and eating children.

Paiyakyamu (Hano Clown) Kachina
Hopi, early twentieth century
(painted and carved cottonwood root)

While most Kachinas represent deeply religious aspects of Hopi or Pueblo cosmology, the clowns are
literally comedians which exist to entertain audiences
during intermissions in ceremonies. The clowns are in
fact often known as Chuchkut, rather than Kachinas.
The playful Paiyakyamu (aka Koshari) symbolizes glut-
tony and overindulgence.

Konin Mana Kachina
Havasupai, late nineteenth century
(painted and carved cottonwood root)

This Konin Mana is a representation of a female
dancer in buckskin and face paint with a buffalo headdress (with one horn missing).

Ketowa Bisena Kachina
Hopi, early twentieth century
(painted and carved cottonwood root)

The Ketowa Bisena is associated with the Bear Clan at the Tewa Pueblo. All Kachinas associated with the Bear Clan are considered to be very powerful entities capable of curing serious illnesses. They appear during the Soyohim (mixed) dances of the springtime.

Tuskiapaya (Crazy Rattle) Kachina
Hopi, early twentieth century
(painted and carved cottonwood root)

The sash and head gear of this figure suggest those of the Tuskiapaya, or Sikyachantaka, Kachina, which appears during times of famine.

Nuvak'chira (Snow) Kachina
Hopi, early twentieth century
(painted and carved cottonwood root)

This representation of the Nuvak'chira depicts the eye panels as yellow and red, representing the north and south rather than white representing the east. The Nuvak'chira is depicted with the white neckpiece and the thunderbolt scepter. Common to many ceremonies such as the Powamu (bean dance) Festival and the Serpent Ceremony, this Kachina represents the spirit governing the snows of winter which dwells atop the San Francisco Mountain Range in north central New Mexico.

Palhik (Polik) Mana Kachina
Hopi, late nineteenth century
(painted and carved cottonwood root)

Female Kachinas were in a decided minority in Hopi culture, but the Palhik Mana was notable. She was variously identified as the Butterfly Girl or the Water Carrying Girl, and is associated with female rites of passage.

Mudhead Kachina Bracelet
Gary Yoyokie (Hopi), 1991
(sterling silver and gold)

'Daydreaming'
Craig Dan Goseyun (San Carlos Apache), 1990
(bronze, 28″ high)

This 28-inch high bronze sculpture was chosen as Best of Show from more than 300 artworks entered in the 1990 Lawrence Indian Arts Show juried competition, and in 1991 it appeared on a poster for the third annual Lawrence Indian Arts Show (Lawrence, KS). The sculpture portrays an Apache woman seated with her legs drawn up and her arms wrapped around her left knee. Goseyun, a professional sculptor with a studio outside of Santa Fe, New Mexico, specializes in bronze and in heavy materials, such as stone, massive blocks of Carrara marble, alabaster and pink marble. He opened his studio after serving six years of apprenticeship to sculptor Allan Houser. 'I'm always learning more about my culture through my work, and I suppose it is taking something out of me,' Goseyun said. 'It really shows me what's inside . . . I'm constantly being taught by my own work.'

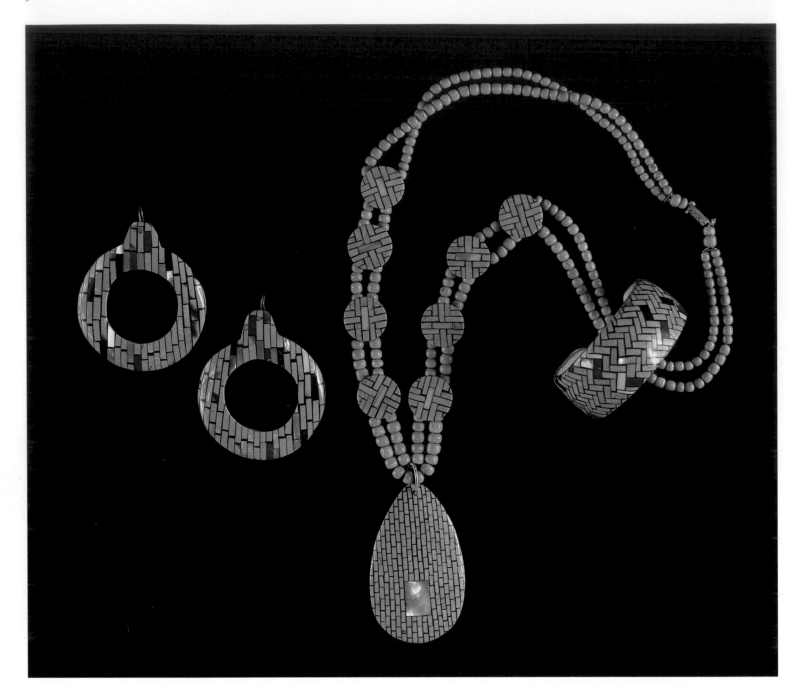

Mosaic Jewelry of Turquoise on Shell
Angie Reano Owen (Santo Domingo Pueblo), c 1991
(Mosaic Turquoise on Shell)

Angie Reano Owen's artistic prowess invoke's an an-cient technique common among Southwestern peoples as far back as 1500 years. Here, Owen accents the mother-of-pearl, lapis lazuli and jet. Trade with Central American tribes provided marine shells and varieties of tropical goods. Courtesy of Gallery 10 Inc, in Scottsdale, AZ and Sante Fe.

Jewelry
Mike Bird (San Juan-Tewa), 1991

Mike Bird's silver-and-gold petroglyph pin, silver snake pin, and earrings with spiny oyster and vericite, is only a glimpse of his unique style as a jeweler on the contemporary scene. Bird combines ancient imagery with elegant originality—giving his work distinctive characteristics and exquisite, colorful charm. Courtesy of Gallery 10 Inc, in Scottsdale and Santa Fe.

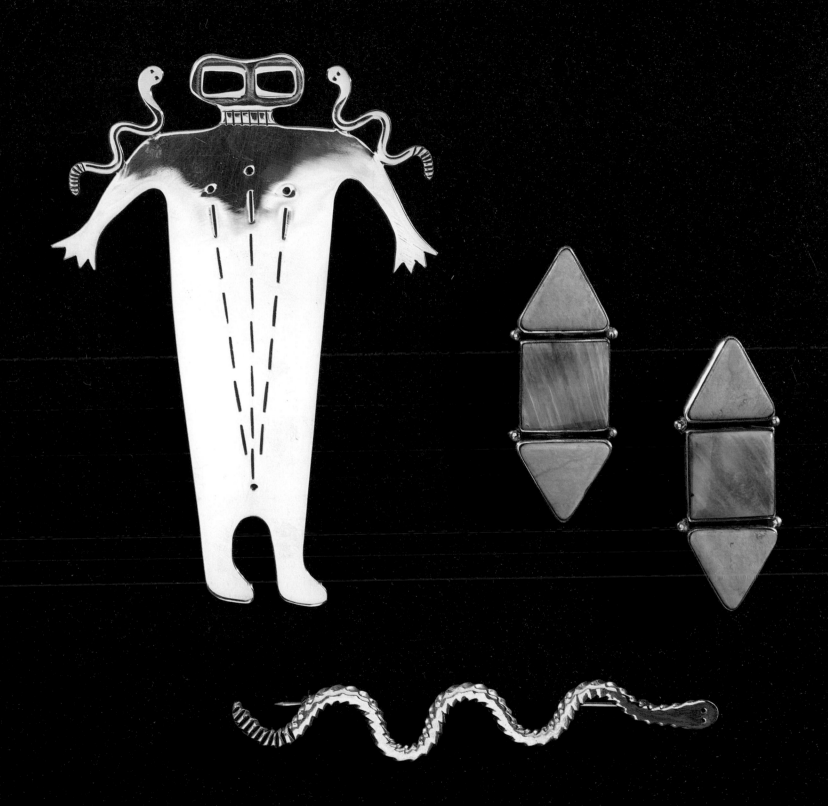

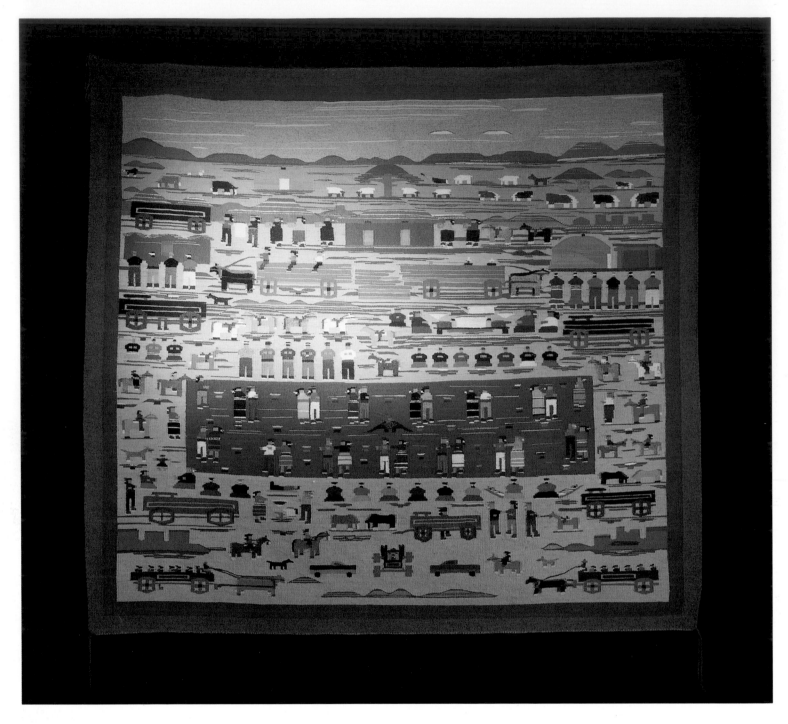

Pictorial Weaving
Juanita Tsosie (Navajo), c 1989
(hand woven, 82″ × 93″)

Known for their unique size and intricacy, Juanita Tsosie's pictorials depict great social gatherings on the Navajo reservation. Pictorials have become one of the most valued forms of American folk art due to the technical difficulty behind their production. Courtesy of Gallery 10 Inc, in Scottsdale and Santa Fe.

Burntwater Weaving
Salina Yazzie (Navajo), 1990
(hand woven wool, 72″ × 48″)

Salina Yazzie is one of many weavers who experiment with plant materials in regions around Burntwater, Arizona. The plants are used for a diverse range of colors, however subtle they may be. In this composition Yazzie uses vegetal-dyed wool yarn. Courtesy of Gallery 10 Inc, in Scottsdale and Santa Fe.

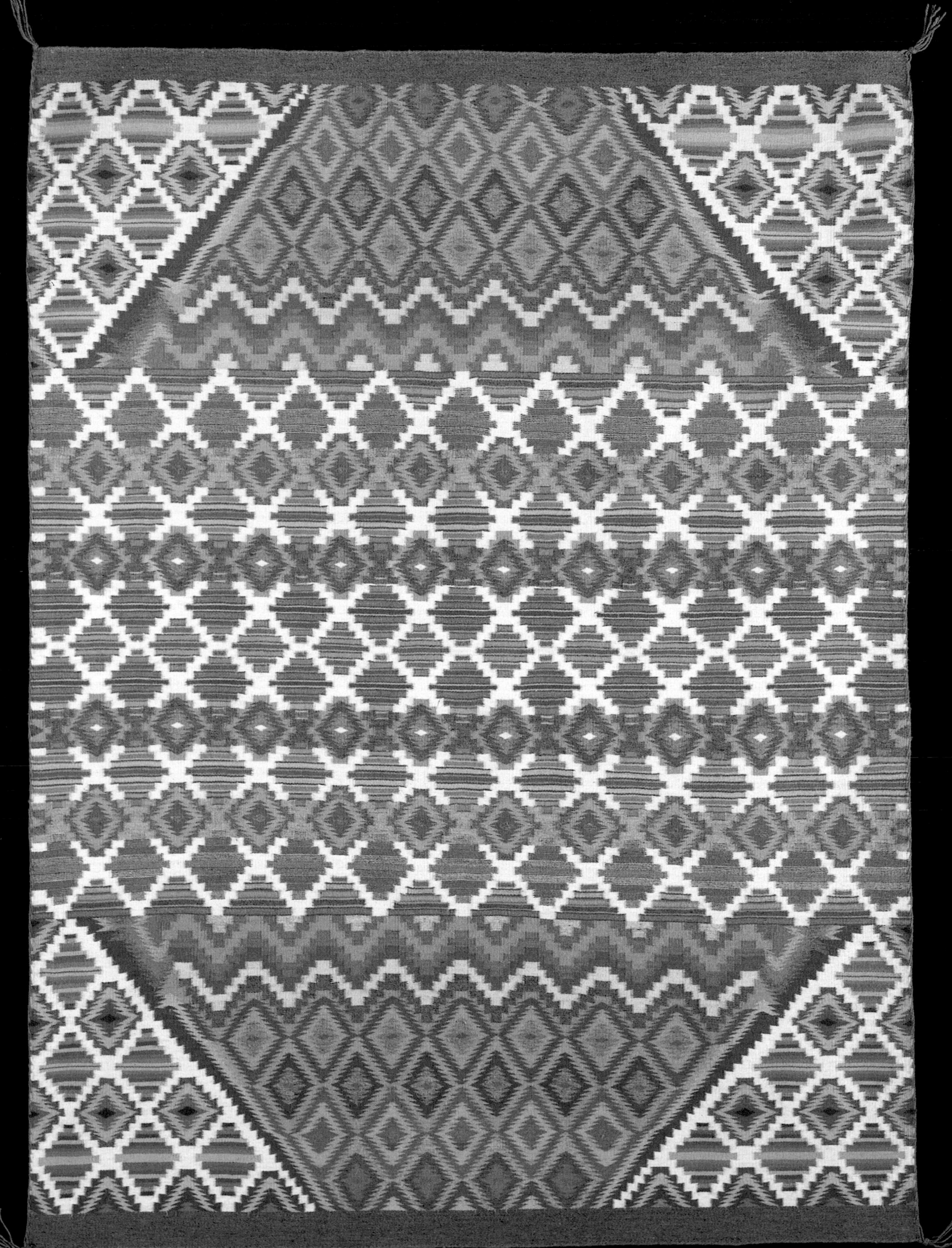

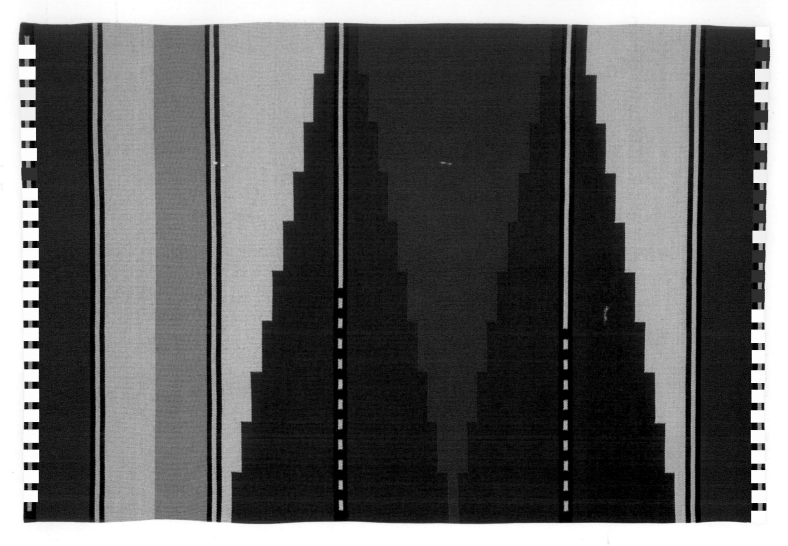

Basket Dance
Ramona Sakiestewa, 1992
(hand woven wool, 50″×75″)

'Some people look for a lot of texture in textile work.
My emphasis is on the color combinations and the per-
fection of the weave. Photo realism, or whatever you
want to call it, just doesn't interest me. I call my work
"American Southwest Tapestry," which means it's drawn
somewhere out of Pueblo tapestry technique.'
    Courtesy of the LewAllen Gallery.

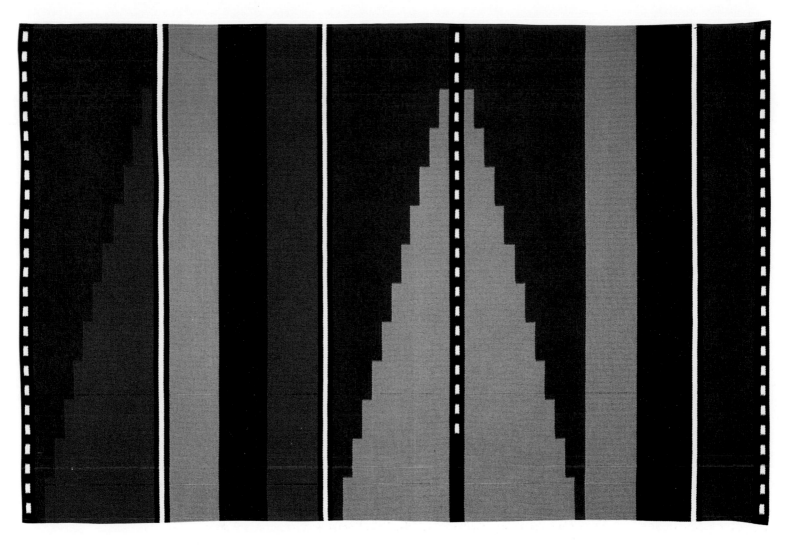

Basket Dance
Ramona Sakiestewa, 1991
(hand woven wool, 50″ × 73″)

Courtesy of the LewAllen Gallery.

Untitled
Jody Folwell (Santa Clara Pueblo), 1982
(ceramics, 12″×9″)

Jody Folwell uses abstract images such as the buffalo, horse and wolf, to pose questions about culture stereotypes for the viewer. Folwell may be asking a specific question—whether these Native American symbols have become symbols of Anglo culture's views of Indian life. Courtesy of Gallery 10 Inc, in Scottsdale and Santa Fe.

Untitled
Jody Folwell (Santa Clara Pueblo), 1986
(ceramics, 12″×9½″)

Jody Folwell graces this asymmetrical piece with Northwest Coast imagery. Folwell's art is exhibited at Gallery 10 Inc, in Scottsdale and Santa Fe.

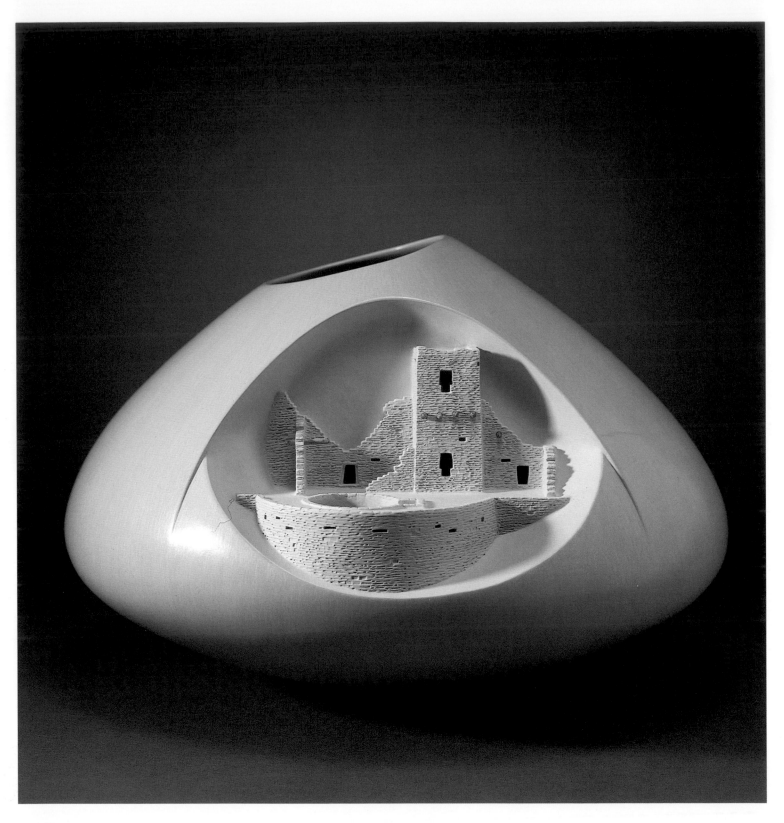

Untitled
Russell Sanchez (San Ildefonso Pueblo), c 1990
(ceramics)

Russell Sanchez has brought together and refined such techniques as burnishing, incising, inlay, two-tone firing, and multiple colors of slip—including a sparkling wash made from micaceous clay. These are some of the techniques an ealier generation of Pueblo potters had introduced in the 1960s. Courtesy of Gallery 10 Inc, in Scottsdale and Santa Fe.

Untitled

Al Qoyawayma (Hopi), c 1989
(hand sculpted, 9″×13½″)

Archeology and engineering are two major influences
in Al Qoyawayma's carved architectural art. Perhaps it is
his aunt Elizabeth White who influenced him the most.
She trained Qoyawayma in the intricate art of extruding
relief elements from inside the pottery wall. Courtesy of
Gallery 10 Inc, in Scottsdale and Santa Fe.

Melon Jar
Nancy Youngblood (Santa Clara Pueblo), 1989
(hand sculpted, 7¼″ × 6⅜″)

Nancy Youngblood's technique gives her art a dramatic sense of proportion, and jewel-like polish. She carries on a tradition passed down from her great-grandmother, Sarafina Tafoya, who used to make jars with swirling ribs in the early twentieth century. Courtesy of Gallery 10 Inc, in Scottsdale and Santa Fe.

Untitled
Nathan Youngblood (Santa Clara Pueblo), 1990
(hand sculpted, 11½″ × 8″)

Elegant, carved storage jars are part of Youngblood's family tradition. His grandmother, Margaret Tafoya used to sculpt the jars in black and red, which set the standard for Santa Clara pottery in the twentieth century. With his precision of carving, complexity of form and contemporary twist, Youngblood keeps the family tradition alive. Courtesy of Gallery 10 Inc, in Scottsdale and Santa Fe.

Never Ending Rain
Anthony Jojola (Isleta Pueblo)
(free-blown glass, 4″×12½″×12⅓″, 15″×9½″×14½″)

Anthony Jojola is one of the leading Native American artists who blow glass into a beautifully designed and colored artistic sculpture. He is said to be 'always looking for new ways to capture the "spirit" of glass and shape it into a contemporary masterpiece.' Mr Jojola works with three other artists in his studio in Santa Fe, NM.

Spirit Offering
Anthony Jojola (Isleta Pueblo) 1992
(free-blown glass, 8½″×13″×8″)

Shield Dancers

Tony Abeyta (Navajo)

(mixed media on canvas, 96″×108″)

Tony Abeyta was raised in Gallup, NM by his Navajo father and European-American mother. He studied art at the Institute of American Indian Art in Santa Fe, Maryland Institute's College of Art in Baltimore and overseas in Southern France and Florence, Italy. He then returned to graduate from the Maryland Institute. Based upon the cultural heroes of the past, mythology and his native culture, Abeyta's canvases are noted for their vivid color. He describes the three dimensional effect as communicating 'the reality and spirituality of the Southwest.'

Night Guardians
Tony Abeyta (Navajo)
(oil and sand on canvas, 50″ × 70″)

'Most of my imagery deals with American Indian
deities;' Mr Abeyta has said 'it's a world that's different,
that tends to be more essential, more pure. I'm more
interested in the icon—the idea—than in painting a
particular deity.'

Wind Canyon Song
Tony Abeyta (Navajo)
(acrylic on canvas, 60″ × 72″)

Mr Abeyta is presently taking post graduate courses in
art and film-making at the Chicago Art Institute. He has
received numerous awards for his paintings and graphic
art.

Homeward Bound
Allan Houser (Houzous) (Chiricahua Apache), c 1989
(bronze)

Allan Houser began his unique and charactaristic style
of sculpting by applying the welding and metalworking
skills he had learned as a pipe fitter in a World War II
shipyard. With this, Mr Houser is said to have set the
course for the future of Native American sculpture. He
has also become an important figure in Native American
stone carving. Allan Houser's work is shown only at the
Glenn Green Galleries in Santa Fe, NM.

3 Taos Men
RC Gorman (Navajo), 1977
(charcoal on paper, 19½″ × 24″)

Rudolph Charles Gorman was born on the Navajo reservation, Canyon de Chelly, AZ in 1932. Known as 'The Picasso of Indian artists', he served in the Navy and attended Northern Arizona University before discovering himself as an artist. He received a grant to study in Mexico and says 'the first time I went and saw Orozco's work, I was stunned. It was so close to my own people. Rivera went to Europe to discover himself. I went to Mexico and discovered Rivera and myself.'

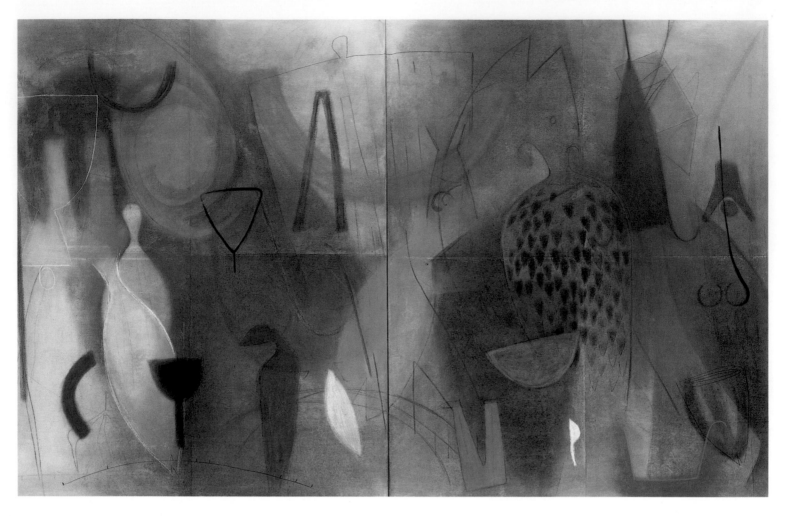

Composition for Scott
Emmi Whitehorse (Navajo), 1990
(oil on canvas, 60″×96″)

Emmi Whitehorse has been committed to her art since she was a child. 'That's all I knew how to do— draw,' she says of her childhood. Courtesy of the LewAllen Gallery.

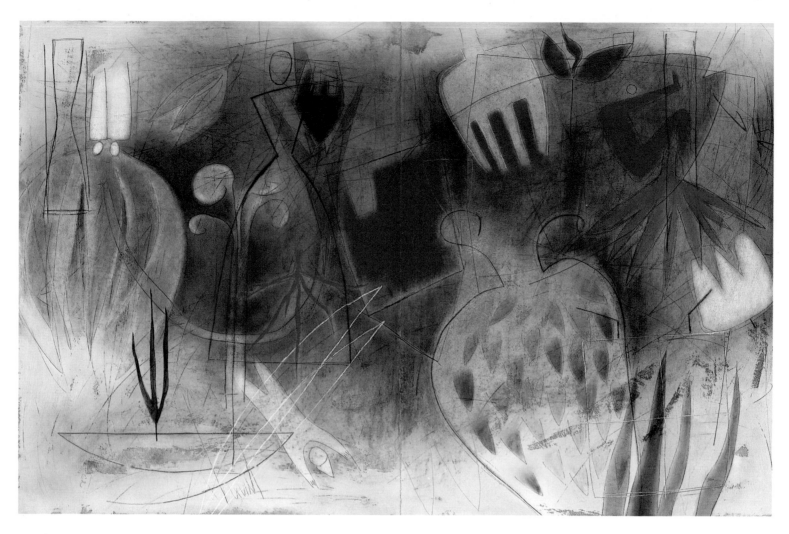

Spring

Emmi Whitehorse (Navajo), 1989
(Oil on paper on canvas, 51″×78″)

"... As I move along in my career, it's like opening a door and stepping into another room," Emmi White-horse says. "I think as a child I knew I could do something with my hands." Courtesy of the LewAllen Gallery.

THE ART AND FOLKLORE OF THE

unters had roamed North America's boundless plains and prairies from about 10,000 BC, following the great buffalo herds on the fast grasslands between the Mississippi River and the Rocky Mountains, from Canada to southern Texas. The hunters came and went, but permanent settlements in the region west of the Mississippi were rare until the second millennium AD. The first native peoples to inhabit the central and western Plains were the Pawnees and Wichitas, who moved from present-day Texas into Nebraska in the 1300s and prospered as farmers. In the north, the Mandan tribe pushed west into the upper Missouri Valley, while the Sioux (Dakota) and Crow migrated from the Great Lakes region and the Blackfoot from Canada, settling on the northern Plains. The Cheyenne moved into the central Plains from the east, and the Comanche came from the Great Basin to occupy the southern Plains.

The loosely organized tribes of the western Plains, such as the Crow, Blackfoot, Arapahoe, Cheyenne and Comanche, were wandering hunters. The eastern Plains tribes, like the Sioux, Omaha and Missouri, were semi-nomadic farmers and hunters who lived in permanent villages between hunts. They

Below: George Catlin painted this view of a Comanche buffalo hunter in the early 1830s. The Comanche were skilled riders and bred their horses for speed and agility.

PLAINS AND BASIN TRIBES

would return to their villages at the beginning of summer, in time for the women to plant crops of corn, squash, beans and tobacco. Once this was accomplished, the tribe departed for a summer of hunting buffalo on the western Plains. In the fall, they returned to harvest their crops and prepare food for storage in concealed, underground pits.

Unlike those of the eastern Plains, tribes of the central and western Plains never farmed, but spent the entire year hunting and traveling on foot in small bands, transporting their portable teepees and belongings on dog-drawn, A-shaped travois. Buffalo hunting was the central focus of Plains Indian culture, and the people's lives revolved around the hunt. The Sun Dance at the end of the summer was a solemn affair for giving thanks to the Sun and seeking the guidance of the guardian spirit for the future. However, its purpose was also to gather the tribe together to prepare for the annual joint tribal hunt. This hunt was strictly organized, and each member had a specific role to play. Scouts preceded the hunting party, warriors kept guard in the rear and police were assigned to maintain order. Women packed the hunters' belongings, in keeping with their roles as managers of the household. In the early days, this tribal

Below: The buffalo was the main source of food and clothing to the Plains Indians. In this 1870 photo of an Arapaho camp by William Soule, buffalo meat is dried on racks and the teepees are covered with tanned buffalo hides.

Above: Sioux warrior Short Bull fought against Custer at Little Bighorn in 1876.

Below: Note the costumes and the teepees in this 1870 photograph of the camp of Shoshone chief Washakie.

Opposite: Chief of the Oglala Dakota Sioux, Red Cloud (Mahpiua-luta) was a respected leader. He led an uprising against the United States for two years which ended in 1868. Note the elaborate breastplates.

hunt was conducted on foot and was an extremely dangerous enterprise during which many lives were lost.

Every part of the buffalo was put to use by the Plains peoples. Hides were tanned and made into teepees, blankets and clothing. Hair was used for weaving. The horns and bones were carved into utensils. Even dried manure pats were used for fuel, and the beast's stomach became a cooking pot. Meat not consumed in the initial feast was hung to dry or pounded with other ingredients into pemmican, or jerky, the food which formed the basis of the Plains Indian diet.

By 1750, thanks to the animals stolen from Spanish conquistadors in the preceding centuries, most Indians on the Plains had become skilled horsemen. Horses vastly improved transportation because they were capable of pulling much heavier loads on the travois than dogs. Hunting was also far easier on horseback. With this new-found mobility, hunting could be accomplished much more quickly, leaving more time for war. Horse raiding became a common activity that lasted for weeks at a time, because possession of horses was a means of gaining wealth and of increasing one's social status in the tribe.

Despite many subtle differences, the daily life and the culture of the Plains tribes were much the same throughout this region. Compared to the tribes of the eastern forests, Plains tribes were loosely organized, bound together only by shared customs. To overcome the language barrier, the Plains Indians developed a basic sign language by using gestures that could be understood by all the tribes. For the most part, ceremonies–which varied from tribe to tribe–were not complex, and attendance was not mandatory. Many tribes had select societies, some based on age and others not, which provided tribal unity by keeping order, preserving and passing on traditions and organizing social life.

The pictorial art of the Plains Indians was less elaborate than art produced in other regions of North America. Painting was popular, but only the men were permitted to paint representational scenes, while women were restricted to geometrical drawings. When glass beads were brought from Europe, Native Americans eagerly traded for them. They loved the bright colors, which were far more vivid than the shells and seeds that were already in use. The beads were much easier to sew and could be applied to entire garments, usually reserved for ceremonial use. Young girls received instructions from their

mothers in traditional arts, such as painting, beadwork and porcupine quill embroidery. Women kept records of their achievements, and during the Sun Dance Ceremony they competed against each other to show off their abilities.

To the west of the Great Plains, between the Rocky Mountains that divide the continent into the Atlantic and Pacific drainage systems, and the Sierra Nevada and the Cascades, lies the Great Basin. It is bounded on the south by the Colorado River and the state of Arizona, and stretches up through Nevada and Utah to southern Idaho, central Oregon and Washington and into British Columbia. The southern part of the Great Basin is a desolate, unforgiving desert, while the northern part, criss-crossed by the great river valleys of the Snake, Columbia and Fraser, is more hospitable.

The people of the southern part of the Basin, principally the Shoshone, Paiute, Ute and Bannock, led an extremely difficult existence in which all their activities, like those of the Athapaskans in the far north, were structured around mere subsistence. Nomadic, they wandered the mountains and valleys of the Basin in search of food. Animal life in the area was also sparse, with jackrabbits being the Indians' preferred fare. They were not only good to eat but their pelts were used to make clothing. These mammals were not always available, however, and the people of the Basin generally depended on mice and insects, especially locusts, for their protein requirements. Berries and pinon nuts were also available but not plentiful.

In order to survive in this barren land, natives had to learn to read and follow the seasons. In the summer, when the blazing Sun parched the valley floor and vegetation became brown and dry, they would climb into the high mountains of the Basin where it was cooler, where plants still flourished and where an occasional kangaroo rat might be found. In winter, when snow came to the high country, they would again return to the valley floor.

The Great Basin peoples had no tribal organization and no permanent social group larger than the family. Sometimes a group of families would unite for as long as wild food was available, but there were no regular festivals or other cultural traditions because of the meager food supply.

However, in the northern part of the Great Basin, life was somewhat easier because of fertile river valleys. This area was

Opposite: Chief Joseph (1830-1904) of the Nez Perce was a noted Native American orator.

Above: Angelica La Moose, whose grandfather was a Flathead chief, is seen here wearing a costume made by her mother. This photograph was taken in northwestern Montana in 1913.

Below: An impressive line of Nez Perce warriors.

also where the Rockies gave way to the lowlands less abruptly, producing a region of intermountain country containing rich lakes and forests. This area includes the mountains and valleys of the Idaho Panhandle and British Columbia, and the great valleys of western Montana, such as the Bitterroot, the Flathead and the McDonald. The Columbia River drainage was home to a number of tribes whose names are familiar as important place names to this day: Spokane, Wenatche, Yakima, Umatilla, Klamath, Okanagon and Walla Walla. The Idaho Panhandle was home to the Coeur D'Alene and Nez Perce, while the Kalispell and Flathead tribes lived in the valleys of northwestern Montana.

These tribes, unlike their cousins to the south, developed a rich cultural diversity through interaction with other tribes from the Northwest coast, California and the Plains. Unlike any of their neighbors except the Plains tribes, they became excellent horsemen. Big game in the form of deer and elk were plentiful, as were fish, wild berries and nuts. Trade flourished within the region and with tribes of neighboring regions.

Notable places in the Plains and Basin areas where artifacts of the ancient native art and culture of the region may be viewed today include: the Glenbow Museum (Calgary, Alberta), the Provincial Museum of Alberta (Edmonton), the Pawnee Indian Village Museum (Republic, KS), the Museum of the Plains Indian (Browning, MT), the Museum of Nebraska History (Lincoln), the North Dakota Heritage Center (Bismarck), the Saskatchewan Museum of Natural History (Regina), the University of South Dakota (Vermillian), Panhandle-Plains Historical Museum (Canyon, TX), and the University of Wyoming Anthropology Museum (Laramie).

THE STORY OF THE THUNDER MEDICINE (A Blackfoot Legend)

It was in the long ago. Our fathers had no horses then, but used dogs to carry their belongings. One spring, needing the skins of bighorn to tan into soft leather for clothing, the tribe moved up here to the foot of the Lower Two Medicine Lake* and began hunting. Many men would surround and climb a mountain, driving the bighorn ahead of them, their dogs helping, and at last they would come up to the game, often several hundred head, on the summit of the mountain. The dogs were then held back, and the hunters, advancing with ready bow and arrows, would shoot the bighorn at close range and generally kill most of them.

One day, while most of the men were hunting, three young, unmarried women went out to gather wood, and while they were collecting it in little piles here and there, a thunderstorm came up. Then one of them–a beautiful girl, tall, slender, long-haired, big-eyed–said, 'Oh, Thunder! I am pure! I am a virgin. If you will not strike us, I promise to marry you whenever you want me!'

Thunder passed on, not harming them, and the young women gathered up their firewood and went home.

On another day, these three young women went out again for firewood, one ahead of another along a trail in the deep woods, and Mink Woman, she who had promised herself to Thunder Man, was the last of the three. She was some distance behind the others and singing happily as she stepped along, when out from the brush in front of her stepped a very fine-looking, beautifully dressed man, and said: 'Well, here I am. I have come for you.'

'No, not for me! You are mistaken. I am not that kind. I am a pure woman,' she answered.

'But you can't go back on your word. You promised yourself to me if I would not strike you, and I did not harm you. Don't you know me? I am Thunder Man.'

Mink Woman looked closely at him and her heart beat faster from fear. But he was good to look at. He had the appearance of a kind and gentle man, and–although thoughtlessly–she had made a promise to him, a god, she could not break it. So she answered, 'I said that I would marry you. Well, here I am. Take me!'

Her two companions had passed on and saw nothing of this meeting. Thunder Man stepped forward and kissed her, then took her in his arms, and, springing from the ground, carried her up into the sky to the land of the Above People.

But the two young women soon missed her. They ran back on the trail and searched on all sides of it, and called and called to her, but of course got no reply. 'She may have gone home for something,' said one of them, and they hurried back to camp.

She was not there. They then gave the alarm, and all the people scattered out to look for her. They hunted all that day and wandered about in the woods all night, calling her name, but got no answer.

The next morning, Mink Woman's father, Lame Bull, made medicine and called in Crow Man, a god who sometimes lived with the people. 'My daughter, Mink Woman, has disappeared,' he told the god. 'Find her, even learn where she went, and you shall have her for your wife.'

'I take your word,' Crow Man answered him. 'I believe that I can learn where she went. I may not be able to get her now, but I will some time, and then you will not forget this promise. I have always wanted her for my woman.'

Crow Man went to the two young women and got them to show him where they had last seen Mink Woman. He then called a magpie to him and said to the bird: 'Fly around here and find this missing woman's trail.'

The bird flew around and around, Crow Man following it, and at last it fluttered to the ground, and looked up at him and said, 'To this spot where I stand came the woman, and here her trail ends.'

'Is it so!' Crow Man exclaimed. 'Well stand just where you are and move that long, shining black tail of yours. Move it up and down and sideways. Twist it in every direction that you can.'

The magpie did as he was told, and Crow Man got down on

*On the east side of Glacier National Park in northwestern Montana

hands and knees and went around, watching the shifting, wiggling, fanning tail. Suddenly, he cried out, 'There! Hold your tail motionless in just that position!' and he moved up nearer and looked more closely at it. The Sun was shining brightly upon it, and the glistening, black feathers mirrored everything around. They were now spread directly behind the bird's body and reflected the treetops, and the sky beyond them. Long, long, Crow Man stared at the tail, the people looking on and holding their breath. At last, he said to Lame Bull, 'I can see your daughter, but she is beyond my reach. I cannot fly there. She is up in sky land, and Thunder Man has her!'

'Ai! Ai! She did promise herself to him the other day if he would spare us,' one of the two wood gatherers said, 'but she did not mean it; she was only joking. It is no joke!'

Lame Bull sat down and covered his head with his robe, and wept, and would not be comforted.

Thunder Man took Mink Woman to sky land with him, and somehow, from the very first, she was happy there with him. She seemed to forget at once all about this Earth and her parents and the people. It was a beautiful land up there: warm and sunny, a country just like ours except that it had no storms. Buffalo and all the other animals covered the plains, and all sorts of grasses and trees and berry bushes and plants grew there as they do here.

But although Mink Woman was very happy there, Thunder Man was always uneasy about her, and kept saying to his people, 'Watch her constantly. See that she gets no hint of her country down below, nor sight of it. If she does, then she will cry and cry, and become sick, and that will be bad for me.'

Thunder Man was often away, and during his absence his people kept a good watch on Mink Woman, and did all they could to amuse her, to keep her interested in different things. One day, a woman gave her some freshly dug *mas*, and she cried out, 'Oh, how good of you to give me these. I must go dig some for myself.'

'Oh, no! Don't go! We will dig for you all that you can use,' the women told her, but she would not listen.

'I want the fun of digging them for myself,' she told them. 'Somewhere, sometime back, I did dig them. I must dig them again.'

'Well, if you must, you must,' they answered, and gave her a digging stick and cautioned her not to dig a very large one, should she find it, for that *mas* was the mother of all the others and was constantly bringing forth new ones by scattering her seed to the winds. She promised that she would not touch it, and went off happily with her digging stick and a sack.

Mink Woman wandered about on the warm grass and flower-covered plain, digging a *mas* here, one there, singing to herself and thinking how much she loved her Thunder Man, and wishing that he would be more often at home. He was away the greater part of the time. Thus wandering, in a low place in the plain, she came upon a *mas* of enormous size. Actually, it was larger around than her body.

'Ha! This is the mother *mas*, the one they told me not to dig up,' she cried, and walked around and around it, admiring its hugeness. 'I would like to dig it, but I must not,' she at last said to herself, and went on, seeking more *mas* of small size.

But she could not forget the big one. She kept imagining how it would look out of the ground, in the lodge, all nicely cleaned and washed, a present for Thunder Man when he should return home.

She went back to it, walked around it many times, went away from it, trying to do as she had been told. But when halfway home, she could no longer resist the temptation. With a little cry, she turned and never stopped running until she was beside it. Then she used the digging stick with all her strength, thrusting it into the ground around and around and around the huge growth, prying up. At last it came loose, and, seizing it by its big top leaves, she pulled hard and tore it from the ground and rolled it to one side of the hole.

What a big hole it was! Light seemed to come up through it. She stepped to the edge and looked down. Upon pulling up the huge *mas*, she had torn a hole clear through the sky Earth! She stooped and looked through it, and there, far, far below, saw—

Why, everything came back to her when she looked through it. There it was, her own Earth land! There was the Two Medicine River, and there, just below the foot of its lower lake, was the camp of her people.

She threw away her digging stick and her sack of *mas*, and ran crying to camp and into Thunder Man's lodge. He was away at the time but some of his relatives were in the lodge, and she cried out to them, 'I have seen my own country, the camp of my people. I want to go back to them!'

Said Thunder Man's relatives to one another, 'She has found the big *mas* and has pulled it up and made a hole in our sky Earth! Now, what shall we do? Thunder Man will be angry at us because we did not watch her more closely.'

Thinking of what he might do to them in his anger, they trembled. They tried to soothe Mink Woman, but she would not be comforted. She kept crying and crying to be taken back to her father and mother.

Thunder Man came home in the evening, and upon learning what had happened, his distress was as great as that of Mink Woman, whom he loved. When he came into the lodge, she threw herself upon him, and with tears streaming from her eyes, begged him to take her back to her people.

'But don't you love me?' he asked. 'Haven't you been happy here? Isn't this a beautiful, rich country?'

'Of course I love You! I have been happy here. This is a good country. But oh, I want to see my father and mother!'

'Well, sleep now. In the morning you will likely feel that you are glad to be here instead of down on the people's Earth,' Thunder Man told her.

But she would not sleep. She cried all night, would not eat in the morning and kept on crying for her people.

Then said Thunder Man, 'I cannot bear to see or hear such distress. Because I love her, she shall have her way. Go, you hunters, kill buffalo. Kill many of them and bring in the hides. And you, all you women, take the hides and cut them into long, strong strips and tie them together.'

This the hunters and the women did, and Thunder Man himself made a long, high-sided basket of a buffalo bull's hide and willow sticks. This and the long, long, one-strand rope of buffalo hide were taken to the hole that Mink Woman had torn in the sky Earth, and then Thunder Man brought her to the place and laid her carefully in the basket, which he had lined with soft robes.

'Because I love you so dearly, I am going to let you down to your people,' he told her. 'But we do not part forever. Tell your father that I shall soon visit him and give him presents. I know that I did wrong, taking you from him without his consent. Say to him that I will make amends for that.'

"You are good, and I love you more than ever. But I must see my people. I cannot rest until I do,' Mink Woman told him, and kissed him.

The people then swung the woman in the basket down into

the hole she had torn in the sky Earth, and began to pay out the long rope, and slowly, little by little, the woman, looking up, saw that she was leaving the land of the sky gods. Below, the people, looking up, saw what they thought was a strange bird slowly floating down toward them from the sky. But after a long time, they knew it was not a bird. Nothing like it had ever been seen. It was coming down straight toward the center of the big camp. Men, women, children all fled to the edge of the timber, the dogs close at their heels, and from the shelter of thick brush watched this strange, descending object.

It was a long, long time coming down, twirling this way, that way, swinging in the wind, but finally it touched the ground in the very center of the camp circle, and they saw a woman rise up and step out of it. They recognized her: Mink Woman! And as they rushed out from the timber to greet her, the basket which had held her began to ascend and soon disappeared in the far blue of the sky.

All the rest of that day and far into the night Mink Woman told her parents and her people about the sky gods and the sky Earth, and even then did not tell it all. Days were required for the telling of all that she had seen and done.

Not long after Mink Woman's return to Earth and her people, Thunder Man came to the camp. He came quietly. One evening, the door curtain of Lame Bull's lodge was thrust aside and someone entered. Mink Woman, looking up from where she sat, saw that it was her sky god husband. He was plainly dressed and bore a bundle in his arms.

'Father! she cried, 'here he is, my Thunder Man!'

And Lame Bull, moving to one side of the couch, made him welcome.

Said Thunder Man: 'I wronged you by taking your daughter without your permission. I come now to make amends for that. I have here in this bundle a sacred pipe, my Thunder pipe. I give it to you and will teach you how to use it, and how to say the prayers and sing the songs that go with it.'

Said Lame Bull to this man, his sky god son-in-law, 'I was very angry at you, but as the snow melts when the black winds blow, so has my anger gone from my heart. I take your present. I shall be glad to learn the sacred songs and prayers.'

Thunder Man remained for some time, nearly a moon, there in Lame Bull's lodge and taught the chief the ceremony of the medicine pipe until he knew it thoroughly in its every part.

'It is a powerful medicine,' Thunder Man told him. 'It will make the sick well, bring you and your people long life and happiness and plenty, and success to your parties who go to war.'

And, as he said it was, so it proved to be a most powerful medicine for the good of the people.

Thunder Man's departure from the camp was sudden and unexpected. One evening, he was sitting beside Mink Woman in Lame Bull's lodge, and all at once straightened up, looked skyward through the smoke hole and appeared to be listening to something. The people there in the lodge held their breath and listened also, and could hear nothing but the chirping of the crickets in the grass outside. But Thunder Man soon cried out: 'They are calling me! I have to go! I shall return to you as soon as I can finish my work.' And with that, he ran from the lodge and was gone. And Mink Woman wept.

Who can know the ways of the gods? Surely not us of the Earth. Thunder Man promised to return soon, but moons passed, two winters passed, and he came not to Lame Bull's lodge and his woman. But soon after he left so suddenly, Crow Man returned from far wanderings and heard all the story of the god and Mink Woman. He made no remark about it, but

spent much time in Lame Bull's lodge. Then, after many moons had passed, he said to the chief one day, 'Do you remember what you once promised me? When your daughter so suddenly disappeared, you promised that if I would even find her, or tell you whither she had gone, you would give her to me when she was found. Well, here she is. Fulfill your promise!'

'But she is no longer mine to give. She now belongs to Thunder Man,' the chief objected.

'Let me tell you this,' said Crow Man, 'You promised to give her to me if I would even tell you where she had gone. I did that. And now, as to this Thunder Man, he will never return here because he knows that I am in the camp, and he fears me. So you might as well give me your daughter now, as you will anyhow later.'

'Ask her if she will marry you. I agree to whatever she chooses to do,' Lame Bull answered.

Crow Man went outside and found Mink Woman tanning a buffalo robe. 'I have your father's consent to ask you to marry me. I hope that you will say yes. I love you dearly. I will be good to you,' he told her.

Mink Woman shook her head. 'I am already married. My man will soon be coming for me,' she answered.

'But if he doesn't come, will you marry me?' Crow Man asked.

'We will talk about that later. I will say now, though, that I like you very much. I have always liked you,' she replied.

More moons passed, and as each one came, Crow Man never failed to ask Mink Woman to marry him. She kept refusing to do so. But after two more winters had gone by and Thunder Man still failed to appear and claim her, her refusals became fainter and fainter, until, finally, she would do no more than shake her head when asked the great question.

Then, at last, in the Falling Leaves Moon of the second summer, when Crow Man asked her again and she only shook her head, he took her hand and raised her up and drew her to him and whispered, 'You know now that that sky god is never coming for you. And you know in your heart that you have learned to love me. Come, you are now my woman. Let us go to my lodge, my lodge which is now your lodge.'

Without a word of objection, Mink Woman went with him. *Ai*! She went gladly! She was lonely and she had for some time loved him, although she would not acknowledge it.

It was a good winter. Buffalo were plentiful near camp all through it, and Crow Man kept the lodge well supplied with fat cow meat. He and Mink Woman were very happy. Then came spring and one day, in new green grass time, Thunder Man was heard approaching camp, and the people went wild with fear. They believed that he would destroy them all as soon as he learned that Mink Woman had married Crow Man. They all crowded around his lodge, begging him to give her up, to send her at once back to her father's lodge.

But Crow Man only laughed. 'I will show you what I can do to that sky god,' he told them, and got out his medicines and called Cold-Maker to come to his aid.

By this time Thunder Man had almost reached the camp and was making a terrible noise just overhead. But Cold-Maker came quickly, came in a whirling storm of wind and snow. Thunder Man raged, shooting lightning and making thunder that shook the Earth. Cold-Maker made the wind blow harder and harder, so that some of the lodges went down before it, and he caused the snow to swirl so thickly that the day became almost as dark as night. For a long time the two fought, lightning against cold, thunder against snow, and little by little

Cold-Maker drove Thunder Man back. He could not face the cold, and at last he fled and his mutterings died away in the distance. He was gone!

'There, I told you I could drive him away,' said Crow Man. 'Mink Woman, you people all, rest easy. Thunder Man will never again attempt to enter this camp.'

And with that, he told Cold-Maker that he could return to his Far North home. He went, taking with him his wind and storm. The Sun came out, the people set up their flattened lodges, and all were once more happy.

Lame Bull retained the pipe that Thunder Man had given him, and found that its medicine was as strong as ever. And from him it had been handed down from father to son and father to son to this day, and still it is strong medicine.

THE STORY OF THE FIRST HORSES* (A Blackfoot Legend)

In that long ago time when the people had only their great, wolf-like dogs for carrying their belongings, there were two very poor orphans, a brother and sister, in the camp. The boy was very deaf, and because he seemed not to understand what was shouted at him, he was believed to be crazy. Not even the relatives of his dead father and mother cared to have him in their lodges. One would keep him for a time and tell him to go, and then another relative would take him in for a short time, and, getting tired of him, send him on to another lodge.

Wherever he went, his beautiful, young sister went with him. Often, in good weather, when camp was moved, the two would stay at the old campground, living on castaway meat so long as it lasted, and then they would overtake the camp and go into the nearest lodge, to at least be sure of a meal.

They were generally barefooted and always shabbily dressed. It was a hard life that they led. Because he was so deaf and believed to be crazy, the boy had not even one playmate in all the camp, nor had his sister, for she knew that it was her duty to be always at his side. There came a time, however, when a childless woman, the wife of a great and rich chief, wanted the girl to raise as her own daughter, and after many days the boy persuaded her to be adopted, but he was left alone and more lonely than ever.

Not long after this separation, the camp moved one day, and the boy, Long Arrow, remained at the old campground to live there as long as he could on the leavings of the people. At last he finished the last scrap of thrown away or forgotten meat and started to overtake the camp. The day was hot, terribly hot, but despite that, the boy traveled as fast as he could, often running, and perspiration streamed from his body and his breath came short and fast in loud wheezes.

Suddenly, while running, he felt something give way with a snap in his left ear, felt something moving out from it, and, reaching up, he pulled from it a long, round, waxy object that looked like a worm.

He held it in his hand and ran on, noting that with his left ear he could plainly hear his footsteps upon the trail. A little later, something snapped in his right ear and began to move out of it, and he took from it another worm-like substance. Keeping both in his hand, he ran on. He could now hear plainly with

both ears and so happy was he that he felt almost as though he could fly.

But that was not all the good that was to come to him that day. Early in the morning, a hunter had left camp with his pack dogs and had taken the back trail in search of buffalo. Just before the boy appeared, he had killed one and was butchering it when he saw the boy approaching him. This hunter, Heavy Runner, was a chief and one of the kindest men in the whole camp. He had long thought to do something for this boy, and now, when he saw him coming, he said to himself, 'The time has come. I shall do something for him!'

The boy came to him and his kill, and he shouted to him, at the same time making signs. 'Sit you down, my boy, and rest. You are wet with sweat and covered with dust. You must be very tired. Take this piece of tripe and eat it. Now let me tell you something. From this day, you are to be my boy. I adopt you. You shall have a place in my lodge, good clothes, a good bed. Try to be good and deserve it all. I am going to try to make a man of you.'

'Heavy Runner, your kind words make me want to cry,' said the boy, his voice trembling, tears dropping from his eyes. He swallowed painfully, brushed away the tears, sat up straight and went on. 'I shall be glad to be your son. I will do all that I can to deserve what you give me. Now, let me tell you something. As I was running away back there on the trail and breathing hard, first in one ear and then in the other, something broke with a snapping noise and out came these two worm-like things, and at once hearing came to me. I believe that I could hear a mouse walking if he were away out there beyond your kill.'

'That is good news and a good sign!' Heavy Runner shouted. He was not yet used to the fact that the boy could hear. Then, remembering, he said more gently, 'You take a good rest while I finish butchering this animal and packing the dogs, and then we'll each take what meat we can carry and go home. Yes, boy, you have a home now, and a good one.'

That evening when Heavy Runner told his woman that he had adopted Long Arrow, she made a great outcry. 'How could you, without asking me, adopt that deaf, crazy boy?' she asked. Then, she cried and said that she would not have him for a son, and ran from the lodge.

People gathered around and pitied her, and said that she was right; the boy was crazy and deaf and worthless, and would not mind, and as soon as he got good clothes, he would run off and again live at old campgrounds.

After a time, she went back to her lodge, and as soon as she entered it Heavy Runner said to her, 'Now, at once, cease your crying, and take the anger from your heart. I have adopted this

---

*The Blackfoot word for horse is Po-no-ka-mi-ta, or literally, 'elk-dog.'

boy, and he is my boy. He is no longer deaf; he was never crazy. He is a good boy, and I shall make a man, a chief of him. See that you treat him well, even if you cannot love him. And believe this: if you do not treat him well, you shall be the one to suffer. Tomorrow morning, begin making some good moccasins for him. I, myself, shall cut out his clothes and he can sew them.'

So began a new life for Long Arrow. If the woman did not love him, she at least treated him well. He did everything he could think of to please Heavy Runner. He went hunting with him and brought home heavy loads of the meat that he killed, and in every possible way was of use to him.

Yet, he was not satisfied. He kept saying to himself, 'I want to do something great for this man who is so good to me.'

Time passed. The boy grew up to be a fine young man, good of heart and of fine appearance. At last Heavy Runner's woman loved him as though he were her own son. But in one thing he was very different from the other young men of the camp: he made no close friends, and when not needed by Heavy Runner, he wandered much by himself. Excepting his sister, whom he frequently took for long walks, he had little to say to anyone, and so the people, all but she and his foster parents, continued to believe him crazy.

One evening he said to Heavy Runner: 'Tell me, what must one do to become a chief?'

'One must be very brave, fearless when facing the enemy and of very kind heart, full of pity for the poor and the old and the sick, and always anxious to help them,' the chief replied.

'Well, I want to become a chief. What is the first thing for me to do?' he asked.

'The first thing to do is to go to some far and dangerous place and get your medicine. That is, something that will make you favored by the gods and bring you good luck in battle and in all matters of life,' Heavy Runner told him.

'That I shall do,' said the young man, 'but first, will you not call in the chiefs and the medicine men and braves and let me hear from them where they went and what they did to get their medicine? I shall then have a better idea of what I am to do.'

'We will have our lodge full of them,' Heavy Runner said. The next morning he shouted out invitations for a smoke, asking only the great of the tribe to come to it. They came, filling the lodge, and then, when the pipe was going the round of the circle, he told why he had invited them to the smoke and asked them to give their experiences in their search for medicines.

One after another, they told their adventures, where they went, what they did, what they saw, what narrow escapes from death they had. And at last it came Spotted Bear's turn. But he refused to share his experience.

'What?' he cried. 'Tell that crazy youth about my adventure? Why, I wouldn't waste my breath on him!'

'But he is a poor boy. He wants to know. You might tell it to him in a short way,' pleaded Heavy Runner.

'I will tell it. Not for his benefit, for he is crazy and would not understand. But I will tell it so that you all may know what I did,' the surly one answered.

'From this very place I traveled southward along the foot of the mountains. Seven days and seven nights I traveled, stopping only now and then for a short rest and sleeping very little, and on the morning after the seventh night, I arrived at the shore of a small lake. There I met a stranger who asked me what I sought, and I told him that I was wandering in search of a strong, powerful medicine.

'"Ah!"' said he, '"in such a matter I cannot help you. Go on south for three days and three nights, and you will find a man who will give you what you seek."

'I went on, stopping only for short rests and rarely sleeping. I traveled south for three days and three nights from that place, and in the morning after the third night, I arrived at a long, wide lake running away back in the mountains. I looked at it, looked at the mountains, turning this way, that way, and when I turned last time, lo! there in front of me stood a man, fierce of face, dressed in strange, beautiful clothing, wrapped in a robe such as I had never seen before, and carrying a spear with a big flint point.

'"What do you here?"' he asked. '"Are you not afraid to come to this, the home of the gods of the deep waters?"

'I answered that I was not afraid, that I feared neither gods nor men, nor any animal of the Earth, the sky or the deep waters. And at that, he cried out, "You are brave. The brave shall be rewarded. Come with me."

'I went with him to his lodge. I am promised to secrecy and dare not tell you where it was. He took me in and fed me, and gave me this robe that I am wearing, this medicine robe, and

taught me the prayers and ceremony that goes with it. I asked him what kind of a robe it was, and he answered that it was the skin of an elk-dog, an animal as large as an elk, and, like the dog, useful for carrying burdens. The gods rode them, he said, and guided them wherever they wanted to go.

'Said I, "May I have one of those elk-dogs to ride home?"'

'"No! They're only for the gods to use,"' he answered, and told me to go.

'I came home. I have the robe. Here it is, proof of all I have told you. And this crazy youth would know where I went, what I did! It is to laugh to think of his going there!'

The pipe went a last round, and then the chiefs, medicine men and braves went home. As soon as they were gone, Long Arrow said to Heavy Runner, 'My chief, you know that I am not crazy. I feel that I must go on an adventure, and I want to go where Spotted Bear went to prove to him that I can go as far and face as many dangers as he did. Will you let me go and keep secret from everyone where I have gone and for what purpose?'

'What you propose is just what I want you to do,' Heavy Runner answered. 'You shall start tomorrow, taking with you all the moccasins and other things you will need, and your foster mother and I will tell no one anything about it.'

At the break of day the next morning, while all the people of the camp still slept, Long Arrow started on his journey of discovery. Straight south he went, by day and by night, resting and sleeping at long intervals, and then only for a very short time. On the third day he arrived at the small lake that Spotted Bear had mentioned, and there met the man of that place, even as he had done.

'What seek you?' the man asked.

'Knowledge. Medicine. The way to become a chief,' Long Arrow answered.

'I cannot help you. Go on south for seven days and seven nights, and you will come to a great lake, and there you will meet a man who can help you, if he cares to do so. It may be that he will not even show himself to you, but anyhow, it is worth your while to go there and try to meet him.'

Long Arrow went on for seven days and seven nights, resting and sleeping less than ever, eating nothing except now and then a piece of dry meat not so large as his hand. Early in the

Below: A sketch by Charles Russell of mounted Blackfoot Indians moving to a new temporary camp. The horse-drawn travois carries their teepees and supplies.

morning after the seventh night, exhausted, hardly able to drag one foot after the other, he came to the great lake, and some distance back from its shore, he laid down on the grass and fell into a sound sleep.

It was late afternoon when he awoke, and, opening his eyes, he was surprised to see a boy standing beside him. He was a beautiful child, by far the most perfect of form and feature that Long Arrow had ever seen. He was so beautiful that it did not seem possible he could be a child of the people of this Earth.

Said the boy to him, 'I have been waiting here a long time for you to awake. My father invites you to his home.'

'I shall be glad to visit him,' Long Arrow answered, and sprang up, put on his weapons and was ready.

The boy led him straight to the shore of the lake and there cried out: 'Do not be afraid. Follow me!' And having said that, changed into a snipe, entered the water and disappeared.

Long Arrow was afraid, terribly afraid of the deep, dark water and the mystery of a place where a child could suddenly become a snipe. But he said to himself: 'If I fail in my search for a medicine, it shall be through no fault of mine,' and he entered the water.

It did not wet him, nor touch him. It parted before him, and he went on down the sloping, sandy bottom of the lake and soon saw, close ahead, a large, fine lodge on which were painted in red and black the figures of two strange animals.

The boy, arrived at the doorway of the lodge, changed suddenly from a snipe back to his natural self and cried out: 'Follow me! Here you will be welcome,' and he went in.

Long Arrow, following him, found himself facing a fine-looking man at the back of the lodge. He was sitting cross-legged on his couch and wore a beautiful, black robe, which entirely covered his legs and feet.

'You are welcome here, my son. Be seated,' said the man, and told his wife to prepare food for his guest.

Long Arrow looked about him. On all sides the lodge was hung with beautiful shields, war clothes, weapons, handsomely painted and fringed pouches of sacred medicines and a porcupine-quill embroidered belt of such brilliant colors that it shamed the rainbow.

The woman of the lodge soon set food before Long Arrow, and, having long fasted, he ate hungrily. The man then filled and lighted a pipe, passed it to his guest, and said, 'I knew that you were coming, and I wondered if you would have the courage to follow my son from the shore of the lake down here to my lodge. Not long ago, a man of your people came here, but he was afraid and would not follow my son. And there he made a great mistake. I was going to give him the most valuable present ever given by gods to men. As it was, I went out to him where he sat far back from the shore and gave him the tanned hide of an elk-dog and sent him home. He was not worthy of a better present. But you are different. I shall give you something of great value. Remain here with us a few days. My son shall show you my band of elk-dogs. You shall hunt and kill meat for us, and when you go, then you shall have the great present.'

The boy went out with Long Arrow and showed him the elk-dogs. They came running from the timber out upon the open prairie at the foot of the lake, and were a wonderful sight. They were far larger than an elk, of shining, black color, had tails of long hair and there was long hair all along the top of their necks and hanging down their foreheads from between their restless ears. They were of all sizes, from suckling young to old males and females, and all were very fat and playful, even the oldest of them.

'Young man of the Earth,' said the boy, 'if you are wise and

watchful, these animals and my father's black robe and his many-colored belt may be your present. The three go together. You have noticed that my father always keeps his feet covered with the black robe, and that when he arises and goes out of the lodge he is very careful to keep the robe lowered around him, like a dragging woman's dress, so that his feet cannot be seen. Well, you have but to see those feet, and anything that you ask for will be yours.'

'I shall do my best to see those feet,' said Long Arrow.

Several days passed. The old people of the lodge were very kind to Long Arrow, and he in turn did his best to please them, hunting most all of the time and bringing in much meat. What time he was not hunting, he would sit close to the herd of beautiful elk-dogs and watch them feed and play. When in the lodge, he watched closely for a sight of the old man's feet, but he ever kept them closely covered.

At last, one evening, the old man started to go out of the lodge, keeping his robe well down upon the ground about him, but as he stepped over the low front of the doorway, his right knee raised the robe and Long Arrow saw his left foot. Lo! It was not a human foot, it was the hoof, the round, hard hoof of an elk-dog!

He gave a cry of surprise at the sight, and the old man, realizing what had happened, exclaimed, 'Hai-yo! How careless of me! Well, it cannot be helped. It must have been fated that he should see it.'

He went on out, and, upon returning, took no pains to conceal his feet. Both of them, and the ankles, were those of the elk-dog.

'You have seen my feet, so you can now tell me what I shall give you,' said the old man as he resumed his seat.

'Don't hesitate; speak right out. Ask for the three things,' whispered the boy.

Long Arrow, taking courage, answered, 'Give me three things: your black robe, your many-colored belt and your elk-dogs.'

'Ha! You ask a great deal,' the old man cried. 'But, because you are brave and good-hearted and not lazy, you shall have the robe and the belt and a part of my band of elk-dogs. The robe and the belt are the elk-dog medicine. Without them, you could never catch and use the animals. There are many prayers and songs and a long ceremony that go with them, and I have to teach it all to you. When you have thoroughly learned them, then you shall go home with your presents.'

Long Arrow was many evenings learning them all, but at last he could repeat every one of them perfectly and dance the dances as well as the old man himself, and finally the latter told him one evening, 'You have done well. I am glad that my elk-dogs and my medicines are to be in your hands. You many start for home tomorrow. And now, listen! Take good heed of what I am about to tell you.

'When you leave here, wearing the black robe and the belt, you are to travel for three days and three nights and never once look back. The elk-dogs will not at first follow you, but on the third day of your homeward journey, you will hear them coming behind you. Even then you must not look back, but keep on walking. After a time they will come on right beside you, and with a rope that I shall give you, you will catch one of them and mount and ride it, and all the others will follow you. They will always do that so long as you have the black robe. Lose that and you lose your animals. They will become wild, and you will never be able to catch and train them.'

'As you say, so shall I do,' Long Arrow answered.

Early the next morning, the old man gave him the robe, the

belt and a rope made from the head hair of buffalo bulls, and he started for home, keeping ever in mind and obeying carefully the old man's instructions. At the time, he had his doubts of the old man. Perhaps a big joke was being played upon him. The elk-dogs would not come on the third day, nor any other day! But he would soon cast off such thoughts, and go on with renewed faith that all would be well with him.

On the third day, he heard behind him the thunder of many hard hoofs upon the hard plain, the occasional whinnying that he had learned to love so well! Then, with an old female leading them, the elk-dogs came close up beside him, and he caught and mounted one of them and rode on.

How happy he was! He realized what this would mean for himself and for the people. These elk-dogs would rapidly increase in number. There would soon be enough of them for all the people, and then they would ride instead of walk, and their lodges and all their belongings would be carried by the animals. And now I can do something for those who have been so good to me,' he said to himself, and rode on, singing the new songs that he had learned.

It was late in the afternoon on the day that he approached the camp. All the men had returned from the hunt. Everyone was outside the lodges, resting in the warm sunshine. The first to discover him gave a shout of surprise and alarm. All the people sprang up and stood gazing at the strange sight. They asked one another what the strange, big, black animals could be? And was it really a man sitting astride one of them?

'It is some fierce god bringing his fierce animals to destroy us!' shouted Spotted Bear, the very man who had so contemptuously used Long Arrow, who had not had the courage to follow the boy-snipe into the water. Again he cried out: 'Surely it is an evil one coming to destroy us!' He fled, and all the people fled with him and took to the brush.

Long Arrow rode into camp and dismounted at Heavy Runner's lodge, and all the elk-dogs came up and crowded around him and the elk-dog he had been riding.

'Heavy Runner! Heavy Runner!' he shouted. 'Be not afraid. I am only your son, come back to you!'

Heavy Runner heard the well-known voice and was no longer afraid. He came hurrying from the brush, all the people

following him, and they all crowded around Long Arrow and his strange animals. Said the youth then, 'Only father and mother that I ever knew, I have brought to you, excepting one female and one male, all these strange and useful animals. As you see, they can be ridden. You will no longer have to walk. Also, they will carry for you everything that is yours. I am glad that I can give them to you, both of you who have been so good to me.'

'How generous of you!' Heavy Runner cried. But his wife could say nothing. She embraced Long Arrow and wept.

'Where did you get the strange black ones?' a chief asked.

'I will tell you all about it this evening. I am cautioned not to talk about the gods in the daytime,' Long Arrow answered.

After picketing the animal he had ridden on good grass and driving the others out from camp, he went into the lodge and rested.

That evening, all the chiefs and warriors came into the lodge, Spotted Bear with them, and he told all about his strange adventures, of his life with the Under-Water People, and how the old man had given him the elk-dogs, the black robe and the belt that he wore. And, of course, he told about Spotted Bear's cowardice in failing to follow the boy-snipe into the water, and how he fled from the lodge, his chieftainship dropping from him as he fled. Never again was he allowed to sit with the chiefs and warriors.

When Long Arrow had finished telling them all about his wonderful adventures, the chief cried out: 'We will move camp to that lake of the Under-Water People. They have more elk-dogs. We will ask for them, give anything to obtain possession of such valuable animals.'

They moved south to the lake but, search as they would, could find no elk-dogs, nor did the boy-snipe nor any of the Under-Water People appear, although the medicine men made sacrifice to them and prayed them to show themselves. They did discover, however, that above this lake was another and longer one, hemmed in by still higher mountains, and so they named the two the Inside Lakes.

---

*These lakes, now known as Upper and Lower St Mary Lake, are on the east side of Glacier National Park in northwestern Montana.

THE OLD MAN AND THE WOLVES (A Blackfoot Legend)

One day, in that long ago time, Old Man was wandering along the edge of this forest, having come over from Cutbank Way. He was feeling very lonely and wondering what he could do to have a more lively time when, as he approached the river here, probably right were we are camped, he saw a band of six wolves sitting on the bank, watching him. He stopped short, watched them for a time and then approached them, calling out, 'My younger brothers! My younger brothers! I am very lonely! Take pity on me. Let me be a wolf with you!'

As I have said, the wolves were six: the father and mother, their two daughters and their sons, Heavy Body and Long Body. The old father wolf answered Old Man. 'Just what do you mean?' he asked. 'Is it that you want me to change you into a wolf, that you want to live just as we do?'

'I want to live with you, hunt with you,' he answered, 'but I don't want to be changed wholly into a wolf. Just make my head and neck to look like yours and put wolf hair on my legs and arms, and that will be about enough of a change. I will keep my body just as it is.'

'Very well, we will do that for you,' said the old wolf. He e took a gray medicine and rubbed it on Old Man's head, neck, legs and arms and made the change.

'There!' said he. 'My work is done. I would like to have made you all wolf, your body as well as the rest of you, but you will do as you are. You are quite wolf-like. Now, let me tell you something about our family. My old wife and I don't hunt much. Your two younger brothers there are the runners and killers and their sisters help in the way of heading off and confusing the game. Your younger brother, Long Body, is the swiftest runner, but he hasn't the best of wind. However, he generally overtakes and kills whatever he chases. Your other younger brother, Heavy Body, is not a fast runner, but he has great staying power, never gets winded, and in the end brings down his game. Now you know them. Whenever you feel like hunting, one or the other of them, as you choose, will go with you.'

'You are very kind to me,' said Old Man. 'I am now very tired, but tomorrow I shall want to hunt with one or the other of them.'

'We are also tired. We have come a long way. It is best that we all rest during this night,' said the old wolf, and he led the way up to the top of a high ridge on the north side of the valley, where they all lay down.

'Why rest out on top of this barren, windy place instead of in the shelter of the timber?' Old Man asked, his teeth beginning to chatter from the cold.

'We never rest in the timber,' the old wolf replied. 'There enemies would have a good chance to take us unawares. Here we can see afar everything that moves, and, as one or another of us is always on watch, we can keep out of danger. Also, we can look down and see the different kinds of game and make our plans to chase what we want, head it off, tire it out and kill it. We always, summer and winter, do our resting and sleeping on high places.'

Before the night was far gone, Old Man became so cold that he trembled all over, and, try as he would, he could not keep his jaws together.

'You annoy us with your tremblings and your teeth chatterings. You keep us from sleeping,' the old wolf complained.

'I shall not annoy you long,' Old Man answered, 'because I shall soon freeze to death!'

The old wolf aroused his wife and children. 'This tender-bodied elder brother of ours is freezing. I suppose we have to protect him. Lie down in a circle around him and cover him with your tails,' he told them.

They did so, and he was soon overcome with heat. 'Take your ill-smelling tails from my body. I am wet with perspiration!' he gasped. They removed their tails and he soon began to shiver. 'Put them back! I freeze!' he cried, and they did as he commanded. During the night he had them cover him many times with their tails and as many times remove them. He passed a miserable night, and so did the wolves, for he kept them from sleeping.

At break of day, all arose, and, looking down into the valley, saw a lone buck mule deer feeding farther and farther away from the timber.

They made a plan for capturing it. They all sneaked around into the timber, and then Long Body and Old Man crept down the valley until the buck saw them and ran, and then they chased it.

Long Body soon pulled it down and Old Man came up in time to seize and break its neck, and felt very proud of himself. The other wolves soon came to the kill, and all feasted. The carcass lasted them two days.

Again and again they went to the top of the ridge to pass the night, and Old Man soon became so used to the cold that he did not need tail covering. When the deer was eaten, they killed another one, and then a buffalo bull, which lasted them some

days. Then, after two failures in chasing antelope and some hungry days, Long Body killed a big bull elk just outside the timber.

They were several days eating it, but at last all the meat and the soft bones were finished, and nothing but the backbone and the hard long bones remained. Said the old wolf, 'We must be saving of what we have left, for it may be some time before we can make another killing. Today we will take turns chewing the upper bone of a hind leg.'

They gathered in a small circle with one of the bones, noses to the center, and the old wolf said to Old Man, 'Now, while this chewing is going on, bone splinters are bound to fly. You must keep your eyes tight shut until it comes your turn to chew, else you many get a splinter that will blind you.

Old Man did as he was told. The old wolf began chewing, and, after gnawing off the end of the bone and getting a little of the marrow, called out to his wife that it was her turn to chew and passed her the bone. So from one to another it went around the circle until Long Body got it and Old Man's turn came next.

His curiosity now got the better of him. He just had to see what was going on and slowly opened one eye, the one next to Long Body. All the wolves had their heads to the ground or resting on their forepaws and all–even Long Body, busily chewing the bone–kept their eyes tight shut.

'Huh! This is a queer way to feast,' Old Man said to himself, and just then a splinter flew from the bone and struck his open eye, not putting it out but causing him great pain and making him very angry. 'I will pay him for that!' he thought, and waited his turn at the bone, becoming more and more angry as he waited.

'Your turn, Old Man,' said Long Body after a time, and passed him the bone. Old Man took it, chewed it for a time, looking sharply at all the wolves. All had their eyes tight shut, so, raising the bone as high as he could, brought it down with all the force of his arm upon Long Body's head and killed him. The other wolves, hearing his twitching as he died, opened their eyes, saw him dead and Old Man staring in horror at what he had done.

'What have you done? You have killed your younger brother!' the old wolf cried.

'I didn't mean to,' Old Man answered. 'When he was chewing the bone, he let a splinter fly and it struck me in this eye. I meant to punish him a little for being so careless, but I did not mean to kill him. I must have struck harder than I thought to do.'

'You had your eyes open! It was your fault that you got the splinter!' the old wolf said, and then he and all the rest began grieving for their dead.

All the rest of that day and all through the night, they howled and howled, and Old Man thought that he would go mad from the mournfulness of it all. He was very sorry and hated himself for what he had done in anger.

The mourning time over, the wolves dug a hole in the ground and buried Long Body and then scolded Old Man. 'Had you killed my son intentionally,' the old wolf concluded, 'we would have had your life in payment for his life. As it is, we will give you one more trail. See that such an accident as that never again occurs!'

'Younger brother,' said Old Man, 'I am grieving and very restless because of what I have done. I want to be moving, to be doing something. Let Heavy Body go with me up in this pine forest and we will try to kill something.'

The old wolf remained silent for some time, thinking, and at last answered. 'Yes, I will allow him to go with you, but remember this: if anything happens to him, we shall hold you responsible and great will be your punishment!'

The two started off, and Old Man said to his partner, 'In some ways, I am wiser than you. I have this to say, and you must heed it: Whatever you start after, be it deer or elk or moose, and no matter how close you may get to it, if it crosses a stream– even a little stream that you can jump–stop right there and turn back. Mind, now, even if a few more leaps will get you to the animal's throat, you are not to make those leaps if it crosses a stream. Should you keep on, death in some form will get you.'

'How do you know this?' Heavy Body asked.

'I may not tell you all that I know,' Old Man replied. 'I have given you the warning. Heed it.'

They went farther up in the timber, and, after some nosing of trails, startled a big bull moose and took after it, Heavy Body running far in the lead. He was fast gaining upon it, was almost at its heels, when it jumped into a wide, long pond–really a widening of the creek–and started swimming across it to an island and from that to the other shore. Heavy Body thought of Old Man's warning, but said to himself: 'He doesn't know everything. I must have that moose!' And into the water he went and started swimming toward the island.

Just as he was nearing the island, a water bear sprang from shore and killed him and dragged him to land. Old Man appeared at the edge of the pond just in time to see the bear and her two nearly grown young begin feasting upon her kill. With a heart full of rage and sorrow, he turned back into the timber and considered how he could avenge the death of Heavy Body.

Two mornings later, just before daylight, Old Man came again to the shore of the pond and close to the edge of the water took his stand and gave himself the appearance of an old stump. Soon after sunrise, the old water bear, coming out from the brush on the island, saw it, sat up and stared at it, and said to herself: 'I do not remember having seen that stump before. I suspect that it is Old Man come to do me harm. I saw him right there when I killed the wolf.'

She stared and stared at the stump, and at last called out to her one of her young. 'Go across there and bite and claw that stump. I believe that it is Old Man. If it is, he will cry out and run when you hurt him.'

The young bear swam across and went up to the stump and bit and clawed it, and hurt Old Man. He was almost at the point of giving up and running away when the bear left him and went back to the island and told the old one that the stump was a stump, nothing else.

But the old one was not satisfied. She sent the other young one over and it bit and clawed Old Man harder than its brother had, but he stood the pain, bad as it was, and that young one went back and also said that the stump was just a common old stump without life.

The old water bear was not yet satisfied. She went across herself and bit and tore at the stump with her claws, and what Old Man had suffered from the others was nothing compared to what he endured from her attack. He stood it, however, and at last, satisfied that her children had been right, that this was a stump and nothing else, she left it and started back for the island.

Then it was that, just as she was entering the water, Old Man picked up the bow and arrows he had made during the two days back in the timber and shot an arrow into her well back in the loin. But the bear dove underwater so quickly he could not see whether he had hit her or not. She swam underwater to the back of the island and went ashore where he could not see her.

He turned and went away back into the timber and slept all the rest of the day and all of the following night.

Early the next morning, Old Man was approaching the pond by way of the stream running from it when he saw a kingfisher sitting on a limb of a tree overhanging the water, looking intently down into it. 'Little brother, what do you there?' Old Man asked.

'The old water bear has been shot,' the bird answered. 'She bathes in the water and clots of blood and pieces of fat escape from the wound, and when they come floating along here, I seize them and eat them.'

'Ha! So I did hit her!' Old Man said. 'How badly, I wonder?'

He went on up the shore of the stream trying to think of some way to get complete revenge for the death of Heavy Body when he heard someone out in the brush chanting. 'Someone has shot the old water bear! I have to doctor the old water bear! Someone has shot the old water bear! I have to doctor the old water bear!'

He went out to see who this might be and found that it was the bullfrog, jumping about and making the chant after every jump. He went to him and asked if the bear was much hurt.

'There is an arrow in her loin,' the frog answered,' and as soon as I find a certain medicine plant, I shall pull the arrow out and apply the crushed plant to the wound. I believe that I can save her life.'

'That you never will,' Old Man said, and fired an arrow into him and killed him. He then took his skin, put it on, tore up a handful of a green plant and swam to the island. As soon as he reached the shore he began chanting as the frog has done: 'Someone has shot the old water bear! I have to doctor the old water bear! And so, chanting and jumping, he followed a trail far into the brush and came upon the old bear and her two young. She was lying on her side, breathing heavily, and her eyes were shut. Old Man bent over her, and, firmly grasping the arrow, shoved it in until it pierced her heart, and she gave a kick and died! He then picked up a club and killed the two young.

'There! That ends the water bear family. I was crazy ever to have made her and her husband!' he exclaimed.

Casting off the frog skin now, he with great difficulty floated the three bears from the island to the shore of the pond. There, a short distance back from it, he found a bowl-shaped depression in the ground. Into this he dragged the carcasses of the bears, after skinning them and taking off all the fat from their meat and insides, and then he tried out the fat and poured the oil over them, completely covering them and filling the depression.

He then called the animals. 'All you who would be fat, come bathe in this oil,' he shouted. And on all sides the animals heard and began to come in. The bears–real bears, the grizzly and the black–came first and rolled in the oil, and ever since that time they have been the fattest of all animals. Then came the skunk, next the badger, after him the porcupine, and all rolled in the oil and got fat. The beaver came and swam across the oil. All that part of him above the water as he swam–his head and the forward part of his back–got no fat, but all the rest of his body– his sides, belly and tail–became extremely fat. Last of all the animals came the rabbit. He did not go into the oil, but, dipping a paw into it, rubbed it upon his back between his shoulders and upon the inside of each leg. That is why he has no fat on other parts of his body.

'Well, there!' Old Man exclaimed after the rabbit had gone. 'I have done some good. I have avenged the death of my wolf partner and have made fat many of my younger brothers!'

Sioux Beadwork
Sioux

   Shown are examples of the excellent beadwork fashioned by the Sioux of South Dakota. These multi-colored medallions come in an infinite number of patterns, and may be purchased on the Reservations where they are made, or in shops across the state.

Ghost Dance Shirt
Sioux, c 1890
(buckskin)

Decorated shirts were worn for the Ghost Dance, during which participants worked themselves into a frenzy and could envision the happy future promised by the Ghost Dance religion. The Ghost Dance originated with the Pauite shaman Wovoka, and quickly spread to other Basin and Plains tribes, proclaiming that a messiah would come and unite all tribes against the whites. The movement died out in the early 1890s when no messiah had yet appeared.

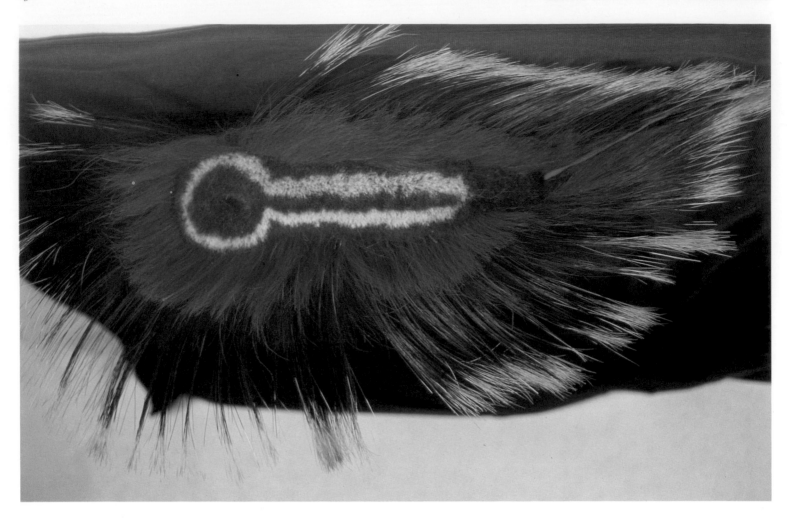

Headdress
Blood, nineteenth century
(deer hair)

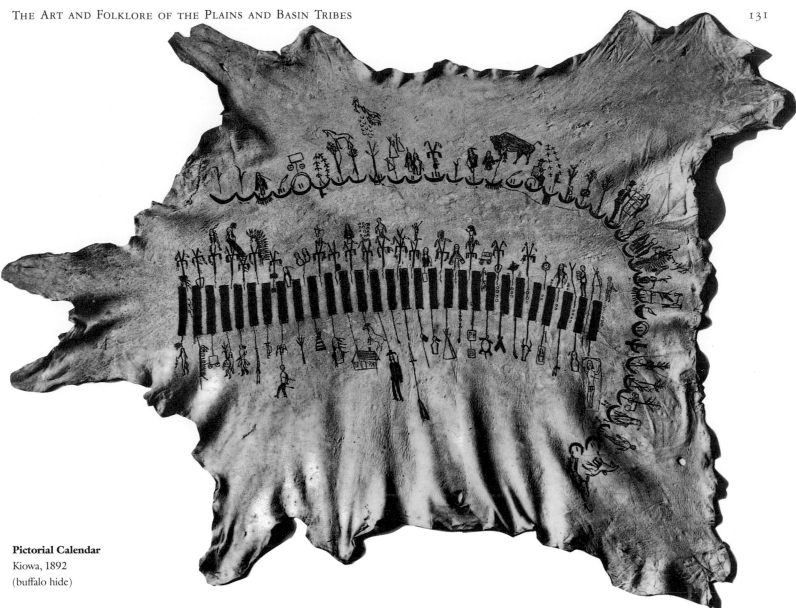

Pictorial Calendar
Kiowa, 1892
(buffalo hide)

This 37-month calendar covers the events of the years 1889 to 1892. Since there was no universal set of symbols, the pictures could not always be understood by those outside the tribe, but the meaning of many symbols is nevertheless obvious.

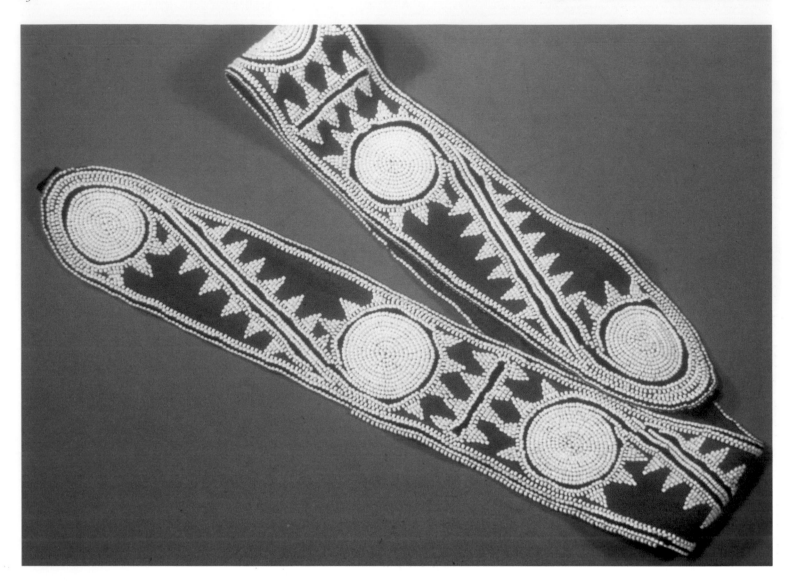

Beaded Sash
Choctaw, nineteenth century
(leather, beads)

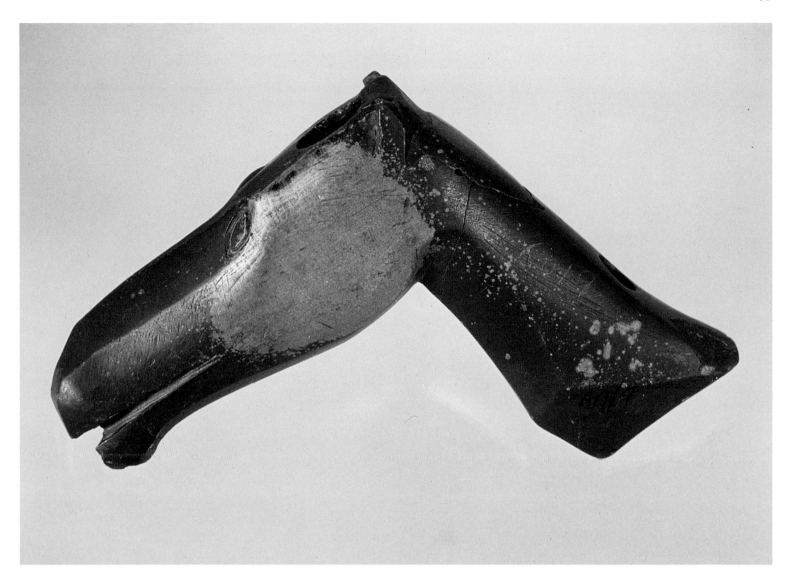

Pipe Bowl
Sioux, c 1840
(carved catlinite)

This pipe bowl was carved in the form of a horse's head, in red pipestone from the sacred quarry. When artist/ethnographer George Catlin returned East, he sent the stone to a geologist for testing, and the new-found mineral was named Catlinite. In the summer of 1836, George Catlin returned to what is now Minnesota to paint the Sioux's sacred quarry, the place of which he had heard so many stories told, where fighting was forbidden. The various Plains tribes came here for red stone that they made into pipes. It was soft enough to carve easily with traditional flint and obsidian tools.

Beaded Pipe Bag (detail)
Sioux, late nineteenth century

Cradleboard

Kiowa, nineteenth century

(wood and rawhide decorated with beadwork)

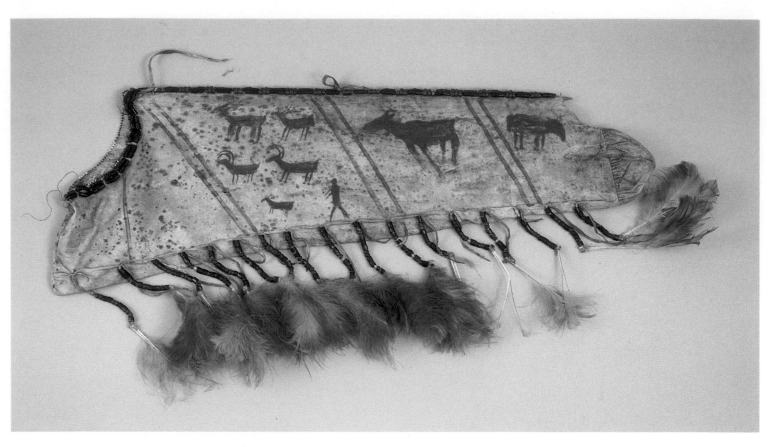

Quiver
Athapaskan, nineteenth century
(Beaded, painted and dyed leather)

Warrior's Headdress
Sioux, c 1890
(eagle feathers, ermine and buckskin)

The feathers in this headdress were rewards for achievements in battle and were incorporated into a war bonnet when a warrior had accumulated a sufficient number. Feathers were cut or marked in a way that indicated the exact deed that had earned them, and in a manner understood by all tribes. This bonnet has been decorated with ermine tails, horsehair and beadwork.

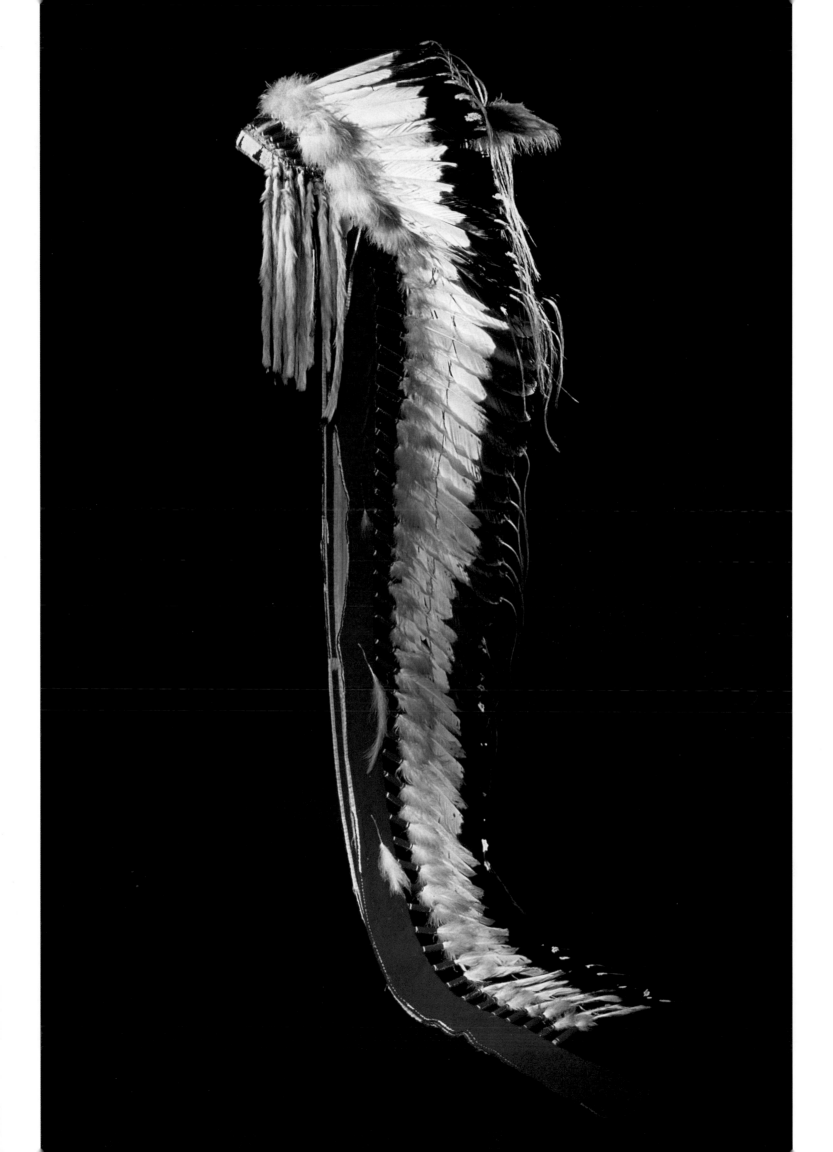

Strange Owl over Summer Camp
Peter Sohappy (Cheyenne)
(hand carved slate, 12″ × 6″)

Peter Sohappy's influence as a sculptor was his grand-mother, who was a folk artist, carving stone for the tribes in Root Digger, Oregon. '. . . It is to my grandparents and their lifestyle I owe my inspiration to create art.' Courtesy of the Moondance Gallery.

The Humpback Flute Player
Peter Sohappy (Cheyenne)
(hand carved slate, 18″ × 9″ × 6″)

Courtesy of the Moondance Gallery.

Moccasins

Dorothy Little Elk (Brule Sioux), 1991

(brain-tanned buckskin, glass beads)

Wapita

Anita Fields (Osage/Creek), 1991

(clay and raku, 2.5″×17″)

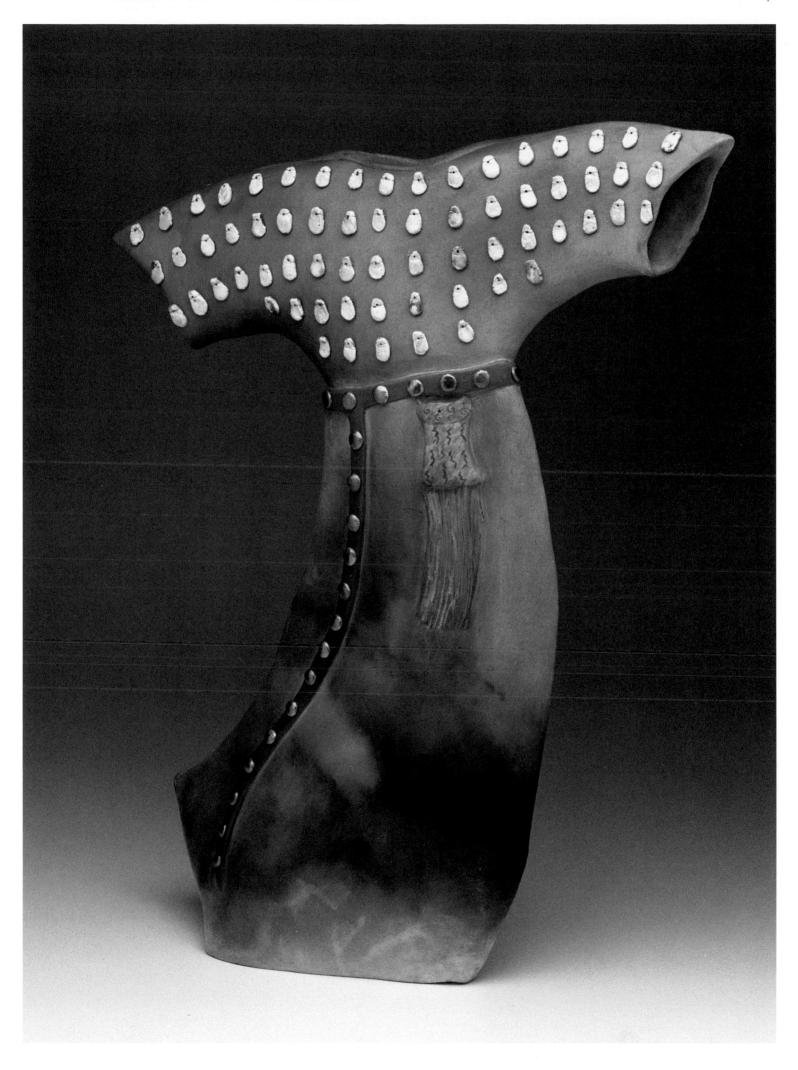

Feral Fire
David D Dubois
(Turtle Mountain Band, Chippewa), 1991
(handmade paper, leather, rabbit)

Ghost Dancer
David D Dubois
(Turtle Mountain Band, Chippewa), c 1990
(leather (cast) circle, 18″)

Cry the Color, c 1990
David D Dubois (Turtle Mountain Band, Chippewa)
(leather circle, 24″)

Mr Dubois does not identify himself as a physical entity, but rather as a 'spirit entity residing within a physical form.' He works in stone, wood, paper and leather. He also paints and makes jewelry.

Hurry Me Home
Bruce LaFountain (Turtle Mountain Chippewa)
(hand sculpted)

Echoes Through Black Canyon
Bruce LaFountain (Turtle Mountain Chippewa)
(hand sculpted,
Belgian marble set with Australian opal and gold leaf
with a marble base, 6' tall)

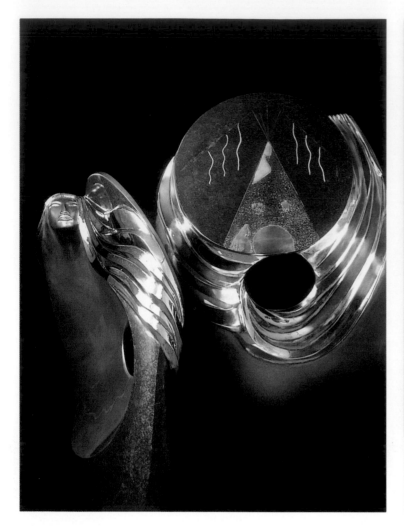

Guardian of the Tipi
Bruce LaFountain (Turtle Mountain Chippewa)
(hand sculpted)

There's a unique blend of many tribes' designs in
Bruce Lafountain's brilliant stone carving. '... What I'm
passing on in my work is a pride in who we are, that our
culture is a beautiful culture, and we're survivors.' Lafountain sculpts his work in his studio in Sante Fe, NM.

Big Water
Bruce LaFountain (Turtle Mountain Chippewa)
(hand sculpted)

Eagle Keeper, Spirit of America
Bruce LaFountain (Turtle Mountain Chippewa)
(hand sculpted, lifesize Utah alabaster)

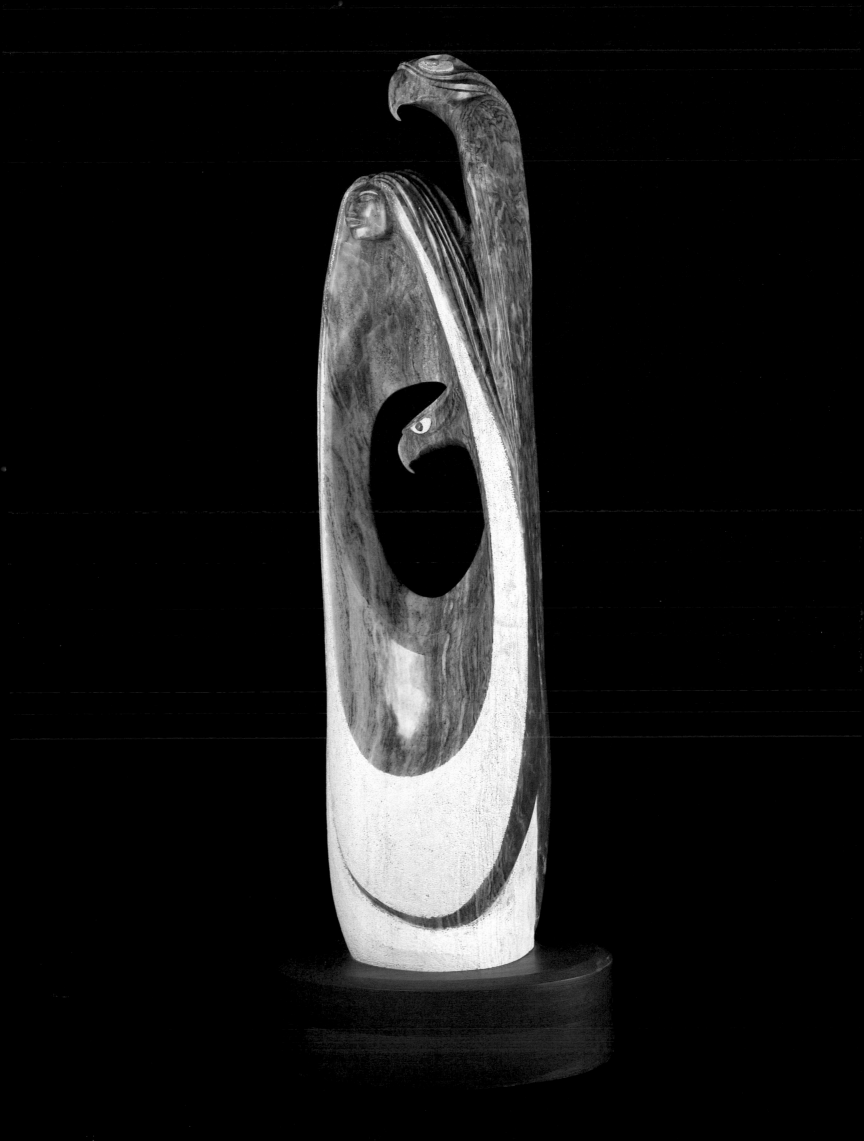

Old Man, Low Mountain
N Scott Momaday (Kiowa, Oklahoma), 1988
(Monotype, 22″ × 30″)

N Scott Mamaday is a poet, Pulitzer Prize winning
novelist, and a self-taught painter, who paints from his
heart and incredibly creative imagination. Mamaday's
work is shown at the LewAllen Gallery.

Environmentalist
N Scott Momaday (Kiowa, Oklahoma), 1991
(Monotype, 30″ × 22″)

'Like a bear, I seem to be blessed with a lot of energy,'
says N Scott Momaday. '. . . One tries to overreach or
outreach one's imagination; to try to astonish God. That
is what I strive for—knowing that I will surely fall short
but, in the process, will always learn something about
myself and my subject.'

Environmentalist

The Spotted Horse
Jaune Quick-to-See Smith
(Flathead tribe, Montana), 1991
(mixed media on paper 30″ × 42″)

Jaune Quick-to-See Smith holds a brush, carefully painting with a political stroke, hoping to convey her message through art. Smith is an activist/spokesperson for contemporary Native American artists. She has founded the Coup Marks on the Flathead Reserve and the Grey Canyon Artists in Albuquerque. Courtesy of the LewAllen Gallery.

Untitled
Jaune Quick-to-See Smith, 1987
(oil on canvas, 60″ × 50″)

Courtesy of the LewAllen Gallery.

Bright Blankets in a Mountain Storm
Earl Biss (Crow), 1992
(oil on canvas, 30″×40″)

Earl Biss' works are on display as part of the permanent collection of the Institute of American Indian Arts Museum, Santa Fe, NM.

Man With Red and White Striped Shirt
TC Cannon (Caddo/Kiowa), 1966
(oil on canvas, 71½″×46″)

Tom Wayne Cannon was born in Lawton, OK on 27 September 1946. He studied at the Institute of American Indian Arts in Santa Fe, San Francisco Art Institute and Central State University in Oklahoma. His one-man shows included American Before Columbus at the Dennis Larkins Gallery in 1970 and Paintings & Graphics at the Southern Plains Museum in 1971. In 1972 Mr Cannon was featured in a two-man show at the Smithsonian Institution in Washington, DC with Fritz Scholder. Tragically, this talented young painter/printmaker died at age 31.

THE ART AND FOLKLORE OF THE

Below: A Kwakiutl village on Hope Island in the Queen Charlotte Straits at the turn of the century. The Northwest Indians evolved a dramatic, distinctive and enormous art form that became their trademark, and is still created today.

The Native American peoples of the Pacific coast, particularly those who lived in present-day Washington, Alaska and British Columbia, enjoyed a relatively sophisticated level of art and culture. These peoples, of whom the major tribes included the Haida, Tlingit, Kwakiutl, Tsimshian, Salish and Chinook, are descended from aboriginal people who made their way to the region as early as 8000 BC. The complexity and refinement of the art and architecture of these peoples was of a level unequaled by any tribe in North America and matched only by the Maya and Aztec in Mesoamerica. They lived in elaborate long houses that were constructed of massive cedar planks without the use of iron tools. They plied the waterways of the area in ornately carved, 65-foot long dugout boats.

CALIFORNIA AND NORTHWEST COAST TRIBES

The quality of their decorative art, chiefly textiles and carving, was on par with much of what was being done in Europe or Asia. The most outstanding examples of the art of carving among the Northwest coast tribes are huge totem poles, which were once proudly displayed next to nearly every house, and which to this day exist in the Indian villages of the Northwest coast. Before 1830, totem poles were uncommon. It is believed the earliest 'totem poles' were structural interior house posts. Next to be developed may have been posts at the exterior corners of clan houses. Detached, exterior poles reached their high point in the late nineteenth century.

Totem poles had no religious significance, contrary to the belief held by many outsiders. Similar poles were carved as built-in supports for a house; others served as poles to hold the ashen remains of a cremated body or as a grave marker for a dead shaman. The shaman was the only member of the Northwest coast society to be buried. All other bodies were cremated.

Traditionally, carving was done by a group of craftsmen who had been formally trained in an apprenticeship system. The totem craftsman was commissioned by the opposite clan when a large totem, house post, or special memorial pole was needed. The desired size, symbols and story were related to him in full detail, and he would then carve a pole according to the specifications. The great height of the totem poles was controlled only by the length of the cedar logs from which they were crafted, and they frequently reached in excess of 50 feet.

Early missionaries to the region were horrified by the totem poles, believing them to be designed to pay tribute to the heathen gods worshipped by these misguided savages. The missionaries, however, were the ones who were misguided in their interpretation of the poles. The name 'totem' is derived from the Algonquian term describing crests showing natural objects or animals that represent a family group. The totem poles were entirely secular, the equivalent of a European crest or coat of arms. In the same way that a European family might select a rampant lion or an eagle to symbolize its view of itself, a Tlingit family or clan might select a bear or raven as its totem animal.

Totem poles were typically found in front of villages belonging to the Haida and Tlingit, or villages in northern British

Above: Hamasoka, principal chief of a late nineteenth century Kwakiutl village, is seen here wearing a blanket decorated with mother of pearl buttons that indicate his status. The buttons were acquired through trade, an economic system common among Northwest tribes.

Columbia and extreme southeast Alaska, and carved house posts were used by the Tlingit. The Haida people were especially skilled at carving the large, wooden, brightly colored totem poles as a bold and proud display of the identity of the inhabitants of a house. Clans named themselves after animals from their mythology which had performed heroic feats, and artists devised stylized symbolic figures to represent each creature, highlighting certain features. No other clan was permitted to use these symbols.

Early Tlingit and Haida poles are usually distinguishable by their layout. Haida figures interconnect and overlap more than the Tlingit figures, which are often isolated from each other and present a more rounded and sculptured appearance. Compared to the Haida, the Kwakiutl tended to use forms directly from nature. They achieved a more three-dimensional effect by carving more deeply into the wood and by attaching wings, horns or plumes to the structures.

Totem poles could contain a whole array of animals representing a legend surrounding that animal, possibly including the huge thunderbird, which lived high in the mountains. The Tlingit and Haida people are each divided into two major groups represented by the raven and the eagle. Within these major divisions were numerous clans that shared legends, crests or symbols, as well as ancestors and artifacts.

Totem poles can be divided into four applications. *Crest* poles give the ancestry of a particular family. *History* poles record the history of a clan. *Legend* poles illustrate folklore or real life experiences. *Memorial* poles commemorate a particular individual.

Totem poles are featured prominently in our view of Northwest coast decorative art, not only because of their size but also because they have been preserved despite their exposure to sunlight and air. Much of the other work carved from the soft

Below: Kwakiutl Shaman Society dancers assemble for a 1914 Hamatsa, or Cannibal Society Dance wearing the wooden hinged masks that represent legendary, as well as real, animals. The long-billed birds represent the Hokhokw, the bird-monsters associated with Bakhbak-walanooksiwey (the Cannibal At the North End of the World). According to legend, the Hokhokw used his long beak to crush human skulls in order to eat their brains.

The Hokhokw were difficult to impersonate, because the mask wearer had to stand up from this position while snapping the heavy cedar beak.

cedar has decayed over time and been lost. Because of this, few Northwest coast artifacts predate the nineteenth century.

Since the cultures in other regions had earlier contact with white people and produced more lasting stone and metal artifacts, our knowledge of them goes back further. The Northwest culture was one of the last to be contacted by Europeans. The east coast of North America was fully settled, Quebec, Boston and New York were thriving cities, and the the great cultures of Mesoamerica had been destroyed by the time white people first made contact with the Indians of the Northwest.

It was not until 1778 that British Captain James Cook actually traded with the Northwest coast people. Even by the time Meriwether Lewis and William Clark arrived in Chinook country at the mouth of the Columbia River, interaction between the Northwest coast tribes and Europeans was still minimal.

The people of the Northwest coast, particularly the Tlingit, were consummate traders. These tribes traded both among themselves and with the tribes on the other side of the coastal mountain ranges. Trading became highly developed because, unlike the tribes in other regions, subsistence required such a small part of their time. Salmon ran in abundance in the

Above: This series of contemporary Tlingit paintings on a public building in Juneau, Alaska, shows traditional Tlingit totem animals with their heads rendered as in native sculpture, and their bodies rendered realistically. From left to right, they are the Raven, the Bear, the Frog, the Eagle, the Killer Whale and the Wolf. Man is shown emerging from a clam shell.

Below: The ornate interior of Tlingit Chief Dlart-Reech's house, as photographed in 1895. Dlart-Reech and his son are lit by a skylight. The boxes flanking them hold treasure for a potlatch. Note that the designs on the boxes are the same as on the back wall. A rain hat such as these worn here is illustrated in color on page 175.

Above, right and opposite: In this series of three photographs showing a Kwakiutl sculptor at work, we see the taking of a slab from a felled cedar tree with a section of the bark removed, the placing of wedges in the sides of the partly split slab and the use of a hafted stone hammer and three mauls.

In the last image, we see the pole begin to take its final, painted form.

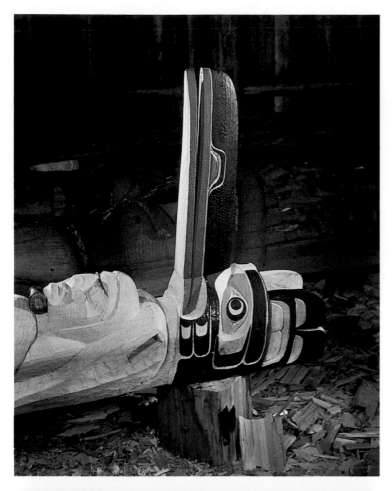

Left: Kwakiutl totem poles on Hope Island, as photographed by CF Newcombe in 1899.

Above: Contemporary Tlingit sculptor Tommy Joseph at work on a carved cedar hat, as photographed in Sitka, Alaska, in 1992.

summer and formed the staple of the Northwest coast diet. Enough salmon could be gathered when in season to last the entire year, thus leaving area natives much time for other activities.

Thus, the accumulation of wealth, as well as artistic pursuits, became a primary preoccupation. Wealth was measured in both material goods and in slaves, the latter being captured farther south among the more docile California tribes. Rank within a tribe was based on affluence rather than heredity, so a low-born person could acquire high rank by amassing possessions. Although religion was not important among the materialistic tribes of the area, shamans did exist, and many became extremely prosperous themselves by charging fees for their unique services.

It was because of this obsession with wealth that the centerpiece of cultural life in the region was a tradition called the Potlatch, which was an enormous party a host gave to celebrate his good fortune. Hundreds of guests would be invited, frequently from two or more clans. Party guests would arrive in their best warships, dressed in their finest costumes, ready for up to 10 days of feasting and general merriment. There would be singing, dancing and toasting of the host and his clan. Rituals were performed, and everyone ate to the point of surfeit.

For the host, however, the Potlatch was a serious event. It was a manifestation of his wealth that he could afford to repeat only a few times–or perhaps only once–in his lifetime, and which might take up to a year of preparation. At the Potlatch, in order to demonstrate how rich he was, a host would give his goods away to show that his holdings were so vast, he could not only throw a huge party, but he could also send his guests home laden with valuable gifts.

Some Potlatch hosts were recorded as giving away thousands of elaborately woven blankets. A man might nearly bankrupt himself hosting a Potlatch, but he would gain much prestige and would soon, of course, be invited to his neighbor's Potlatch, where he would himself receive many gifts.

With the rapid influx of white traders in the latter part of the nineteenth century, however, the character of the Potlatch changed. Mass-produced blankets took the place of those that took months of handwork to complete. Worst of all, the white man began to take a dim view of the Potlatch, and it was outlawed in Canada in 1884. The ceremony continued as an underground activity until well into the twentieth century, but eventually died out, although the ban was officially rescinded in 1951.

Notable places in the Northwest coast area where artifacts of the ancient native art and culture of the region may be viewed today include: the British Columbia Museum (Victoria, BC), Sgan Gwaii, an uninhabited Haida village in the Queen Charlotte Islands; the University of British Columbia Museum (Vancouver, BC), the Portland Art Museum and Oregon Historical Society (Portland, OR), the Makah Cultural and Research Center (Neah Bay, WA) and the Burke Museum at the University of Washington (Seattle).

The area present-day California south of the Siskiyou Mountains near the present-day Oregon border, west of the Cascades near the present Nevada border, and north of the Mohave Desert, is a temperate land with good soil and cyclically sufficient rainfall. This land was home to a polyglot of diverse peoples who migrated here migrated many centuries ago. A large population developed, but probably because of the many incompatible languages, there was little interaction among tribes.

Above: Contemporary Tlingit basket-maker Teri Rofkar
at work on a cedar bark basket. The dark-colored high-
lights are woven using a special sub-species of maiden
hair fern. The cedar bark is kept wet while being braided
in order to insure that it remains pliable.

Opposite: In this series of photographs demonstrating
the creation of Yakima basketry, we see Mrs Campbell
stripping cedar bark and her use of an awl. In the photos
at the bottom, Mrs Campbell makes a wicker work
foundation of cedar bark and finally she adds bear grass
to the sides of the wicker foundation.

The people of the major language families in northern California–the Pomo, Yurok, Yokut, Shasta, Hupa and Miwok–
subsisted on acorns, berries, wild game and fish from streams,
while the Chumash of southern California used 25-foot canoes
to seek out a supply of ocean fish vital to their diet. The natives
of California did not build towns or cities like their neighbors in
the Northwest and Southwest, and their ceremonial life was, as
near as can be ascertained, on a much smaller scale than that
found in any part of the continent except the Great Basin. One
might note, however, that the ancient Shasta people of north
central California had a strong attachment to the spiritual
importance of Mt Shasta (see *How Old Man Above Created the
World*), a belief that has been shared by many adherents to the
New Age movement of the late twentieth century.

The native peoples of California first encountered the white
man in the form of the Spanish conquistadors, and later Spanish missionaries, who transplanted a good deal of their culture
and religion to the new land. The first of a chain of missions was
established at San Diego in 1769, and by 1776 the chain of
Spanish missions ranged up the coast (a day's ride apart) to San
Francisco. In contrast to the more warlike tribes of the Plains
and elsewhere, many of California's Indians willingly became
mission Indians, working at the missions and gradually adopt-
ing the more elaborate Hispanic culture. The result was that by
the time Spanish rule ended in the 1820s, the Indian population had been decimated by European diseases and the elements of its culture lost.

Notable places in the state of California where artifacts of the
ancient native art and culture of the region may be viewed
today include: Adan Treganza Anthropology Museum at San
Francisco State University, the Lowie Museum of Anthropology at the University of California in Berkeley, the San Diego
Museum of Man, the Southwest Museum (Los Angeles) and
at Kule Loklo, a reconstructed Miwok village located about an
hour north of San Francisco.

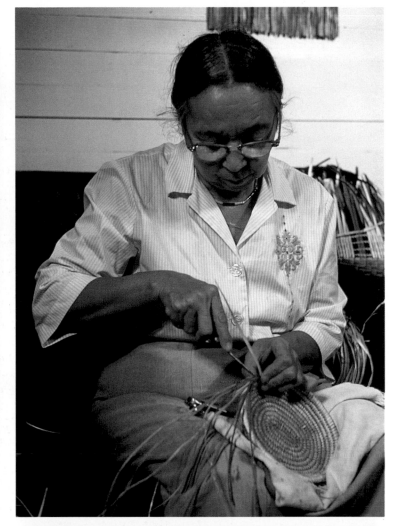

HOW OLD MAN ABOVE CREATED THE WORLD (A Shasta Legend)

Long, long ago, when the world was so new that even the stars were dark, it was very, very flat. Chareya, Old Man Above, could not see through the dark to the new, flat Earth. Neither could he step down to it because it was so far below him. With a large stone, he bored a hole in the sky. Then through the hole he pushed down masses of ice and snow, until a great pyramid rose from the plain. Old Man Above climbed down through the hole he had made in the sky, stepping from cloud to cloud, until he could put his foot on top of the mass of ice and snow. Then, with one long step, he reached Earth.

The Sun shone through the hole in the sky and began to melt the ice and snow. It made a hole in the ice and snow. When it was soft, Chareya bored with his finger into the Earth, here and there, and planted the first trees. Streams from the melting snow watered the new trees and made them grow. Then he gathered the leaves which fell from the trees and blew upon them. They became birds. He took a stick and broke it into pieces. Out of the small end he made fishes and placed them in mountain streams. From the middle of the stick, he made all the animals except the grizzly bear. From the big end of the stick came the grizzly bear, who was made master of all. Grizzly was large and strong and cunning. When the Earth was new, he walked upon two feet and carried a large club.

So strong was Grizzly that Old Man Above feared the creature he had made. Therefore, so that he might be safe, Chareya hollowed out the pyramid of ice and snow as a teepee. There he lived for thousands of snows. The Indians knew he lived there because they could see the smoke curling from the smoke hole of his teepee. When the paleface came, Old Man Above went away. There is no longer any smoke from the smoke hole.

White men call the teepee Mount Shasta.

THE ORIGIN OF LIGHT (A Miwok Legend)

In the earliest beginning, the darkness was thick and deep. There was no light. The animals ran here and there, always bumping into each other. The birds flew here and there, but continually knocked against each other.

Hawk and Coyote thought a long time about the darkness. Then Coyote felt his way into a swamp and found a large number of dry tule reeds. He made a ball of them. He gave the ball to Hawk, with some flints, and Hawk flew up into the sky, where he touched off the tule reeds and sent the bundle whirling around the world.

But still the nights were dark, so Coyote made another bundle of tule reeds, and Hawk flew into the air with them and touched them off with the flints. These reeds were damp and did not burn so well.

That is why the Moon does not give so much light as the Sun.

CREATION OF THE HUMAN RACE (A Miwok Legend)

After Coyote had completed making the world, he began to think about creating man. He called a council of all the animals. The animals sat in a circle, just as the Indians do, with Lion at the head, in an open space in the forest. On Lion's right was Grizzly Bear, next Cinnamon Bear and so on to Mouse, who sat at Lion's left.

Lion spoke first. Lion said he wished man to have a terrible voice, like himself, so that he could frighten all animals. He wanted man also to be well covered with hair, with fangs and very strong teeth.

Grizzly Bear laughed. He said it was ridiculous for anyone to have such a voice as Lion, because when he roared, he frightened away the very prey for which he was searching. But he said man should have very great strength, that he should move silently but very swiftly and he should be able to seize his prey without noise.

Buck said man would look foolish without antlers. A terrible voice was absurd, but man should have ears like a spider's web and eyes like fire.

Mountain Sheep said the branching antlers would bother man if he got caught in a thicket. If man had horns rolled up, so that they were like a stone on each side of his head, it would give his head enough weight to butt very hard.

When it came Coyote's turn, he said the other animals were foolish because they each wanted man to be just like themselves. Coyote was sure he could make a man who would looked better than Coyote himself, or any other animal. Of course, he would have to have four legs, with five fingers. Man should have a strong voice, but he need not roar all the time with it because he could then stand erect when he needed to. Grizzly Bear had no tail and man should not have any.

The eyes and ears of Buck were good and perhaps man should have those. Then there was Fish, who had no hair, and hair was a burden much of the year.

Coyote thought man should not wear fur. And his claws should be as long as the Eagle's so that he could hold things in them. But no animal was as cunning and crafty as Coyote, so man should have the wit of Coyote.

Then Beaver talked. Beaver said man would have to have a tail, but it should be broad and flat so he could haul mud and sand on it. Not a furry tail, because they were troublesome on account of fleas.

Owls said man would be useless without wings.

But Mole said wings would be folly. Man would be sure to bump against the sky. Besides, if he had wings and eyes both, he would get his eyes burned out by flying too near the Sun.

But without eyes, he could burrow in the soft, cool Earth where he could be happy.

Mouse said man needed eyes so he could see what he was eating. And nobody wanted to burrow in the damp Earth. So the council broke up in a quarrel.

Then every animal set to work to make a man according to his own ideas. Each one took a lump of earth and modeled it just like himself.

All but Coyote, for Coyote began to make the kind of man he had talked of in the council.

It was late when the animals stopped work and fell asleep. All but Coyote, for Coyote was the most cunning of all the animals, and he stayed awake until he had finished his model. He worked hard all night.

When the other animals were fast asleep, he threw water on the lumps of Earth and so spoiled the models of the other animals. But in the morning, he finished his own and gave it life long before the others could finish theirs.

Thus man was made by Coyote.

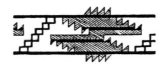

THE FIRST MAN AND WOMAN (A Yurok Legend)

The first man created by Coyote was called Aikut. His wife was Yototowi. But the woman grew sick and died. Aikut dug a grave for her close beside his campfire, for the Nishinam did not burn their dead then. All the light was gone from his life. He wanted to die so that he could follow Yototowi, and he fell into a deep sleep.

There was a rumbling sound and the spirit of Yototowi arose from the Earth and stood beside him. He would have spoken to her, but she forbade him, for when an Indian speaks to a ghost he dies. Then she turned away and set out for the dance-house of ghosts. Aikut followed her. Together they journeyed through a great, dark country, until they came to a river which separated them from the Ghost-land. Over the river there was a bridge of but one small rope, so small that hardly Spider could crawl across it. Here the woman started off alone, but when Aikut stretched out his arms, she returned. Then she started again over the bridge of thread. And Aikut spoke to her, so that he died.

Thus together they journeyed to the Spirit-land.

THE THEFT OF FIRE (A Karok Legend)

There was no fire on Earth, and the Karoks were cold and miserable. Far away to the east, hidden in a treasure box, was fire which Kareya had made and given to two old hags, lest the Karoks should steal it. So Coyote decided to steal fire for the Indians.

Coyote called a great council of the animals. After the council, he stationed a line from the land of the Karoks to the distant land where the fire was kept. Lion was nearest the Fire-land, and Frog was nearest the Karok land. Lion was the strongest and Frog was the weakest, and the other animals took their places, according to the power given them by Man.

Then Coyote took an Indian with him and went to the hilltop, but he hid the Indian under the hill. Coyote went to the teepee of the hags. He said, 'Good evening.'

They replied, 'Good evening.'

Coyote said, 'It is cold. Can you let me sit by the fire?'

So they let him sit by the fire. He was only a coyote. He stretched his nose out along his forepaws and pretended to go to sleep, but he kept the corner of one eye open, watching. He spent all night watching and thinking, but he had no chance to get a piece of the fire.

The next morning, Coyote held a council with the Indian. He told him when he, Coyote, was within the teepee, to attack it. Then Coyote went back to the fire. The hags let him in again. He was only a coyote. But Coyote stood close by the casket of fire. The Indian made a dash at the teepee. The hags rushed out after him, and Coyote seized a fire brand in his teeth and flew over the ground. The hags saw the sparks flying and gave chase. But Coyote reached Lion, who ran with it to Grizzly Bear. Grizzly Bear ran with it to Cinnamon Bear. He ran with it to Wolf, and at last the fire came to Ground-Squirrel. Squirrel took the brand and ran so fast that his tail caught fire. He curled it up over his back and burned the black spot in his shoulders. You can see it even today.

Squirrel came to Frog, but Frog couldn't run. He opened his mouth wide and swallowed the fire. Then he jumped but the hags caught his tail. Frog jumped again, but the hags kept his tail. That is why Frogs have no tail, even to this day.

Frog swam underwater and came up on a pile of driftwood. He spat out the fire into the dry wood, and that is why there is fire in dry wood even today. When an Indian rubs two pieces together, the fire comes out.

THE FOXES AND THE SUN
(A Yurok Legend)

Once upon a time, the Foxes were angry with Sun. They held a council about the matter. Then 12 Foxes were selected–12 of the bravest–to catch Sun and tie him down. They made ropes of sinew, and then the 12 watched until the Sun, as he followed the downward trail in the sky, touched the top of a certain hill. Then the Foxes caught Sun and tied him fast to the hill. But the Indians saw them and they killed the Foxes with arrows. Then they cut the sinews. But the Sun had burned a great hole in the ground. The Indians know the story is true because they can see the hole which Sun burned.

THUNDER AND LIGHTNING
(A Maidu Legend)

Great-Man created the world and all the people. At first the Earth was very hot, so hot it was melted, and that is why even today there is fire in the trunk and branches of trees and in the stones.

Lightning is Great-Man himself coming down swiftly from his world above, and tearing apart the trees with his flaming arm.

Thunder and Lighting are two great spirits who try to destroy mankind. But Rainbow is a good spirit who speaks gently to them and persuades them to let the Indians live a little longer.

Arrow and Spear Points
Shasta, nineteenth century
(flaked obsidian)

Left: Members of the Hupa tribe from Humboldt County, CA, assemble for the White Deerskin Dance in the 1890s. Albino deerskins, like the ones shown here, were the most valuable, and ownership of them indicated high social status. This festive dance was one of two that comprised the second part of the World Renewal Ceremony and followed the sacred ritual. The Hupa chiefs in the foreground carry the sacred obsidian knife and wear headdresses made of sea lion teeth. The longer teeth were of greater value.

Dancers wore costumes provided by wealthy members of the tribe. The more elaborate costumes indicated the affluence and community status of the individual donor. These were made of deerskin or civet cat skin. The dancers, bedecked in shell necklaces and with feathered headdresses covering their eyes, carried poles brandishing the full skins of deer, complete with stuffed heads and legs still attached.

Arrow and Spear Points
Shasta, nineteenth century
(flaked obsidian)

Sewing Implements, Tools
Yokut, nineteenth century
(carved bone)

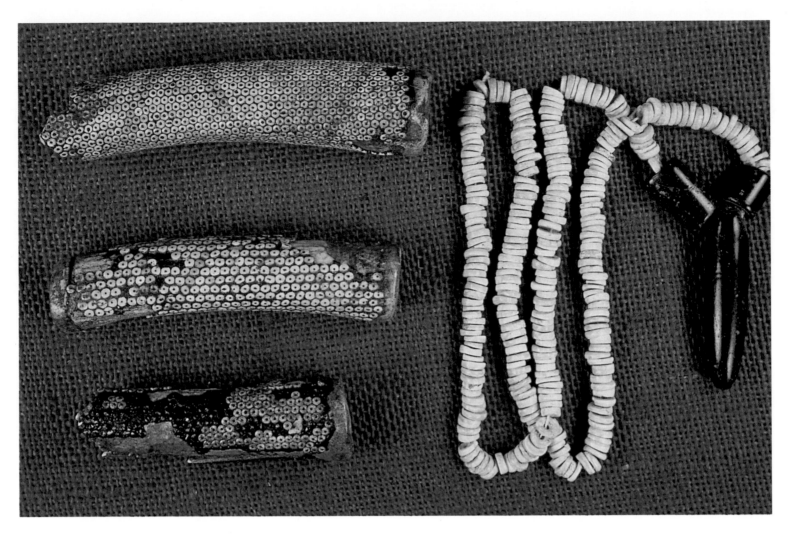

Necklace and Jewelry
Yokut, nineteenth century
(shell beads, bone, antler)

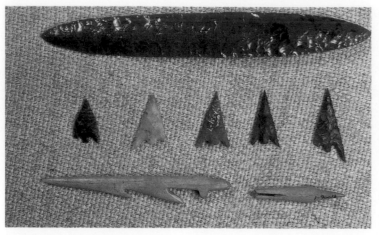

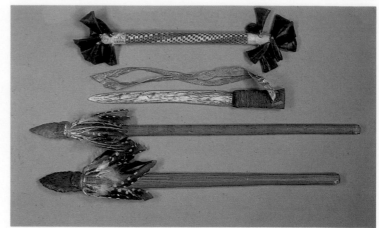

Scrapers and Arrow Points
Yurok, nineteenth century
(flaked obsidian)

Fishing Implements
Yurok, nineteenth century
(carved bone)

Deer Hoof Rattle
Yurok, nineteenth century
(bone, leather, deer hooves)

Dance Wand
Yurok, nineteenth century
(bone, leather)

Ceremonial Spears
Yurok, early twentieth century
(wood, feathers, flaked obsidian)

Moccasins
Modoc, late nineteenth century
(beaded buckskin)

Basket
Yokut, nineteenth century
(woven reeds)

Two Baskets
Yokut, nineteenth century
(woven reeds)

Our Happy Times
Dat-So-La-Lee (Washoe), c 1920
(willow basket)

The artist was born in 1835 at a Washoe village near
Lake Tahoe, NV, and died at Carson City, NV in 1926.
She learned basketry as a child, but did not begin making
handmade baskets for commercial sale until 1895. Her
work came to national prominence after the 1919 St
Louis Arts & Crafts Exposition, and by 1921 her baskets
were being sold for as much as $5000.

Baby Cradle
Mono, late nineteenth century
(willow and leather)

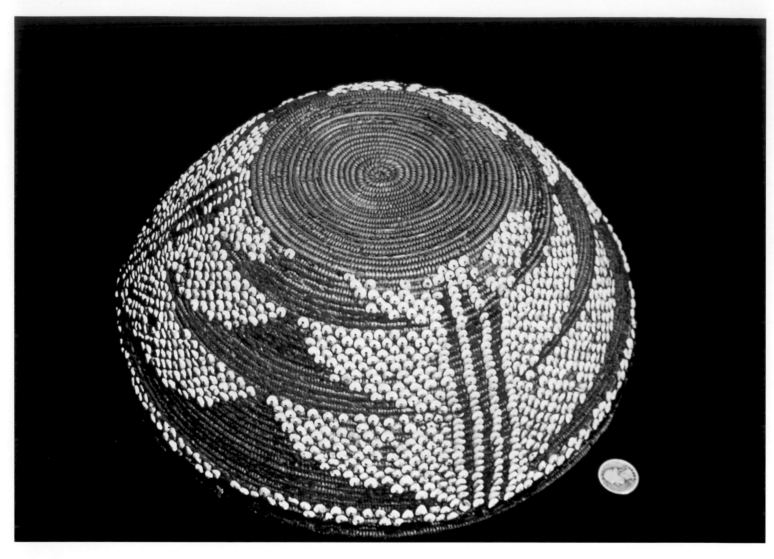

Coiled Basket
Costanoan, nineteenth century
(woven reeds with shell beads)

Gift Basket
Pomo, c 1890
(woven reeds decorated with feathers and shell beads)

Otta with Lid and Water Bottle
Mohave, late nineteenth century
(woven reeds, ceramic)

Flute and Doll
Mohave, late nineteenth century
(woven bark, carved wood)

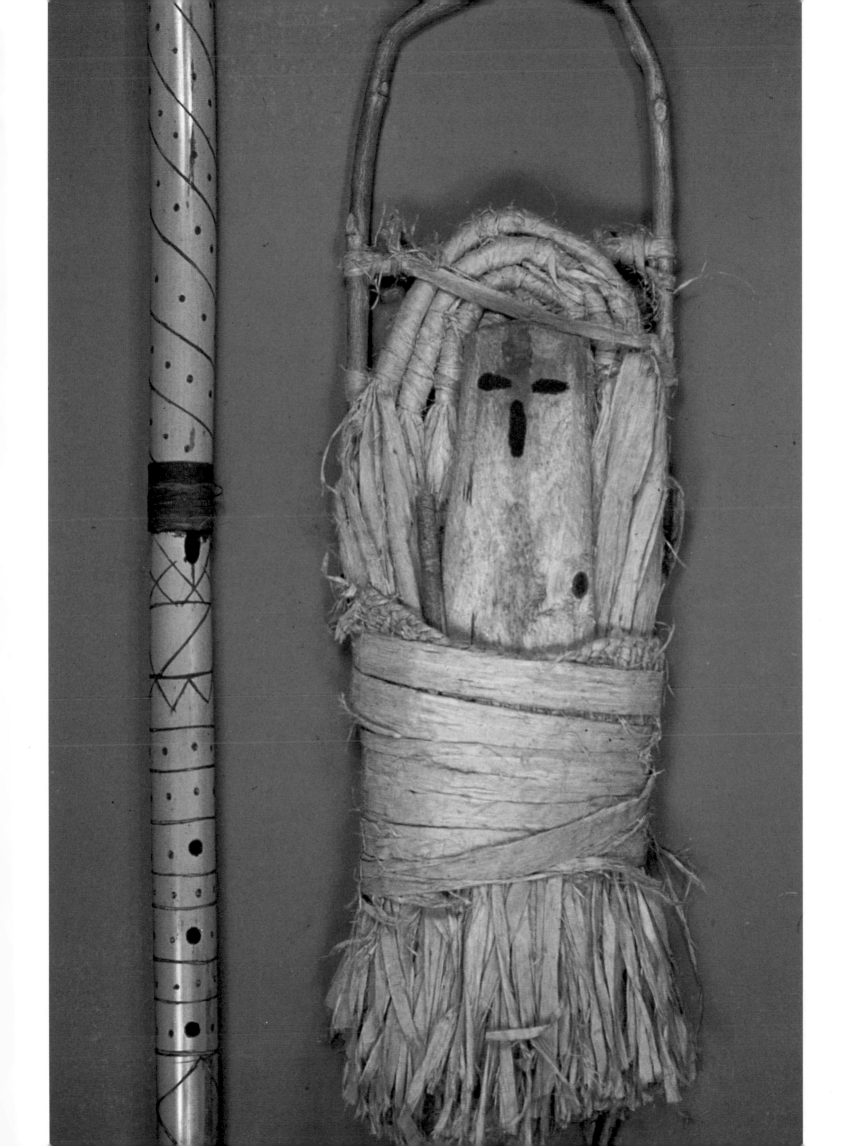

Ceremonial Mask
Kwakiutl, nineteenth century
(carved and painted cedar)

Chilkat Dress
Tlingit, early twentieth century
(woven mountain goat wool)

Chilkat Blanket

Tlingit, early twentieth century
(woven mountain goat wool)

Eagle Feast Bowl
Kwakiutl, c 1870
(carved cedar)

Rain Hat
Haida, c 1880
(woven spruce root, 7"×16.5")

Fetish
Tlingit, late nineteenth century
(carved and painted cedar)

Feast Spoon Representing a Sea Lion
Tlingit, early nineteenth century
(carved mountain sheep antler)

Tools, Hafted Hammerstone and Three Mauls
Kwakiutl, nineteenth century
(carved stone, wood)

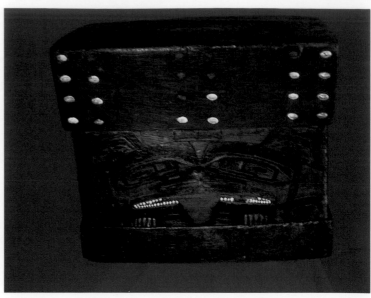

Storage Box
Kwakiutl, nineteenth century
(carved red cedar, opercula inlay)

Storage Box
Kwakiutl, nineteenth century
(carved red cedar, operala inlay)

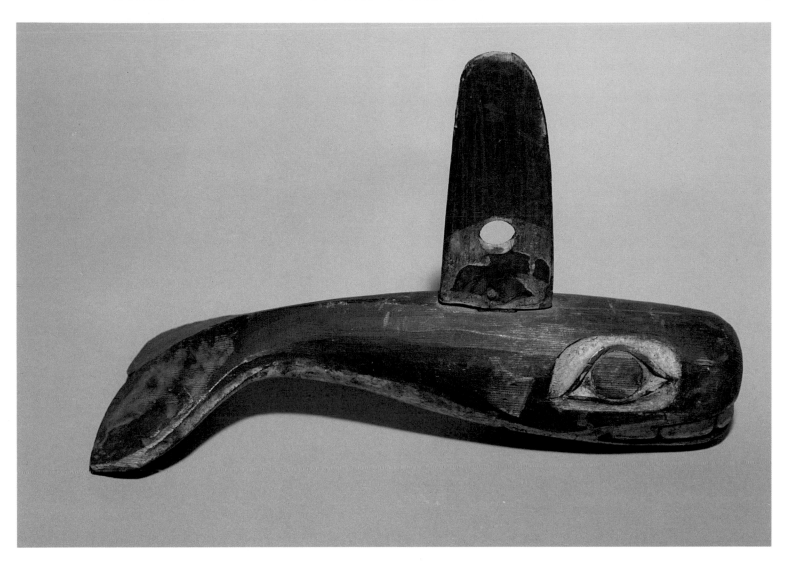

Killer Whale Crest Figure
(from a grave post)
Haida, nineteenth century
(carved and painted cedar)

Owl (?) (Totem pole detail)
Tsimshian, c 1870
(carved, but heavily weathered, cedar)

Mawdzeks Bird (Totem pole detail)
Tsimshian, c 1870
(carved, but heavily weathered, cedar)

Raven (Totem pole detail)
Tsimshian, c 1870
(carved, but heavily weathered, cedar)

These carvings are crests of household groups, and are from poles that stood in front of a house of the Laxsel clan in the village of Kitwancool in British Columbia. They had been exposed to the elements for over 90 years when they were rescued in 1962.

Yaadaas Corner Totem Pole (detail)
Haida, late nineteenth century
(carved cedar)

    This pole is from the Dzeilu house in Kasaan village.
The bear, seen here, is a symbol of transference of knowledge. The bear and raven are both totems identified with
the Yaadaas clan at Kasaan.

**Yaadaas Corner Totem Pole
(detail of a person eating an otter)**
Haida, late nineteenth century
(carved cedar)

Frog/Raven Totem Pole
Haida, late nineteenth century
(carved cedar)

    This Sukkwan village crest pole, now at Sitka, is named
for two of the Northwest Coast's most important totem
animals.

Sisiutl Grave Marker
Kwakiutl, early twentieth century
(carved cedar)

The Sisiutl was a legendary two-headed sea serpent that could transform itself into many different creatures and inanimate objects. A favorite, according to legend, was the form of a slow-moving canoe that had to be fed with seals to prevent a hapless observer from being killed by the Sisiutl. It liked to kill and eat humans, but if properly favored, it might protect one's house. As such, the Northwest peoples often painted its image on the ends of long houses.

Hokhokw (Bird-monster) Mask
Kwakiutl, 1894
(carved and painted cedar with attachments)

Hokhokw masks were worn by the Kwakiutl Shaman Society dancers in the Hamatsa, or Cannibal Society Dance. These long-billed bird-monsters (similar in representation to the raven) were associated with Bakhbak-walanooksiwey (the Cannibal At the North End of the World). According to legend, the Hokhokw used his long beak to crush human skulls in order to eat the brains. The Hokhokw masks were difficult to use because they were heavy and required delicate balancing. The one seen here is 59 inches long.

**Articulated Transformation Mask in the shape of
an Eagle (closed)**
Kwakiutl, nineteenth century
(carved and painted cedar)

These carved masks, used for storytelling ceremonies,
were often of two or three parts. The exterior mask was
attached with hinges and was opened at the right moment in the story to reveal an interior mask (*facing page*).

**Articulated Transformation Mask in the shape of
an Eagle (opened to show a human face)**
Kwakiutl, nineteenth century
(carved and painted cedar)

Totem Pole (detail)
Tlingit, late twentieth century
(carved and painted cedar log)

Totem Pole
Tlingit, late twentieth century
(carved and painted cedar log)

Petals Dancing

Laura Wee Lay Laq (Salish and Kwa-guilth), 1988
(ceramic, 8½″×14″)

'For me, clay not only allows me to express my hopes
and fears but also gives me an opportunity to feel at one
with nature,' says Laura Wee Lay Laq of her artistic
prowess. 'Clay gives me a sense of harmony and peace.'
Courtesy of the Bellas Artes Gallery, Santa Fe.

Blue Indian on Red Sands

Fritz Scholder (Mission), 1968
(oil on canvas, 60″×72″)

Fritz Scholder was born in Breckenridge, MN on 6
October, 1937. He studied at the University of Kansas,
Wisconsin State University and Sacramento City Col-
lege with Wayne Thiebaud. He then went on to earn a
BA at Sacramento State University and an MFA at the
University of Arizona. He has also received several hon-
orary doctorates, including one from the Salon D'Au-
tomne in Paris, France.

In 1972 Mr Scholder was featured in a two-man show
with TC Cannon at the Smithsonian Institution in
Washington, DC. The veteran of numerous one-man
shows, Mr Scholder has also appeared in several Public
Broadcasting Service films, including *Fritz Scholder* and
Fritz Scholder/An American Portrait.

Courtesy of the Institute of American Indian Arts
Museum, Permanent Collection, Santa Fe, NM.

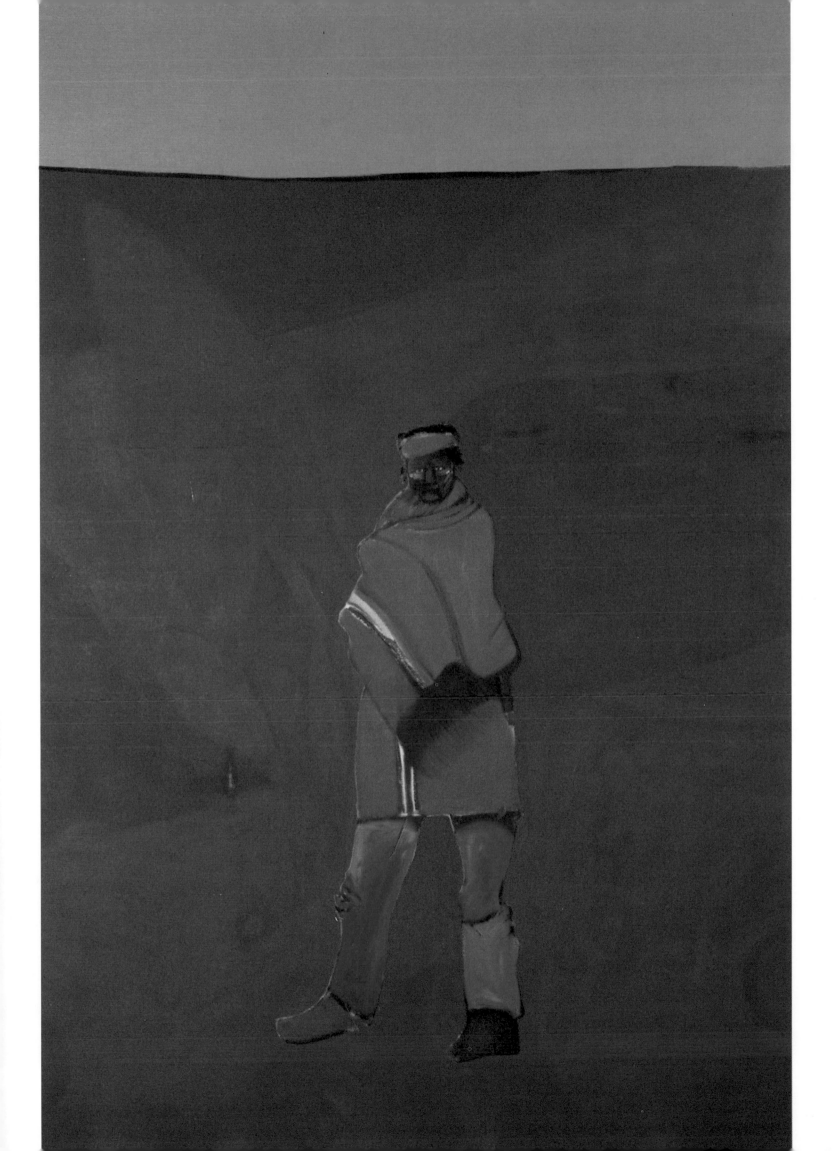

THE ART AND FOLKLORE

Above: An Inuit mother and her child, as photographed in Alaska by HG Kaiser in 1915.

Nowhere in North America are the effects of severe weather on the culture of a people felt more deeply than among the peoples of the Arctic, some of the most rugged territory in the world. Given the name Eskimo, or 'eaters of raw flesh,' by the Algonquians tribe to the south, the natives of the Arctic refer to themselves as Inuit, which simply means 'the people.'

The ancestors of all North American Indians passed from Asia via the now long-gone Bering Land Bridge, through central Alaska and through Inuit country, and very solid archaeological evidence shows that the ancestors of today's Inuit were living in Alaska in 3000 BC.

In other regions of the continent, an area as vast as that populated by the Inuit–6000 miles across–would be home to tribes speaking a multitude of languages, most likely from several linguistic groups. However, from eastern Siberia to the coast of Greenland, the Inuit language is, with some minor local variations, the same.

The life of the people of this vast, homogenous culture is a continuous struggle against the natural environmental forces, from the biting cold of the arctic winter to the mosquitoes of summer.

Nonetheless these people have adapted well, becoming as much an integral part of this harsh ecosystem as the seal and walrus upon whom they depend for their livelihood–more so than on other birds and animals, such as gulls and foxes, which are merely seasonal visitors to the Far North.

When the night of the arctic winter descends upon this region, the Inuit's life turns inward to small villages consisting of one-room houses. The Inuit houses of Alaska and Siberia are usually semi-subterranean wood or earthen structures, but the inhabitants of northern Canada and the islands of the Arctic Ocean north of Hudson Bay often live in traditional ice houses known as igloos. In these, they remain quite comfortable amid piles of polar bear and musk ox hides, spending long winter nights socializing in their compact homes in the flicker of whale-blubber-fueled soapstone lamps, while arctic gales howl outside.

The centerpiece of winter villages (in spring, families go their separate ways for the summer months) is a ceremonial igloo where community festivities take place.

OF THE ARCTIC PEOPLE

The seal is the Inuit's staple game animal, and appears frequently in their art and folklore. Hunting during the winter is a difficult, though not insurmountable, chore. Known as 'puiji,' or 'those that show their noses,' seals are hunted through the very holes in the ice through which they show their noses. Because it is a mammal, the seal must come up for air, and is then vulnerable to hunters. The Inuit traditionally hunt with spears, but nets are also used to trap seals. In the last century, more sophisticated harpoons, as well as guns, have become part of the hunter's arsenal. While the men hunt, women care for the home. Both whales and walruses are also important to the Inuit, not only for food but also for ivory, which is used for tools and ceremonial purposes. In the spring and summer months, birds return to the Arctic and become part of the Inuit diet.

Few cultures have as strong a belief in the supernatural, or such a high per capita number of shamans (medicine men), as the Inuit. Dietary laws are particularly important in their pantheon of beliefs. For example, mixing the flesh of land and sea animals is strictly forbidden.

When seals or whales are killed, they are ceremonially given a drink of water so they will go back to the spirit world and report that they were treated with respect. Future seals and whales can then confidently allow themselves to be killed by the same hunter. A polar bear's spirit remains on the spear that killed it for five days, so its skin must be kept inside for that time. The shamans, who maintain the delicate balance between the natural and spirit worlds, were once ordinary hunters who discovered they had a special gift of extraordinary powers. They were empowered to heal the sick by chasing away demons and, by locating stolen souls, returning them to the bodies of their owners.

The bulk of Inuit art has consisted of carvings, all of which have been done by men. Simple tools are used to shape ivory, bone, horn or wood with great care and a delicate touch. The objects are often small and the simple designs abstract, geometrical or representational of animals from daily life.

To the south of the region inhabited by the Inuit lie the vast, flat steppes of northern Canada and central Alaska. This immense tundra, scraped bare by the enormous glaciers of the ice age, is home to peoples of two distinct linguistic groups. To the

Above: During their 1913-1918 expedition to the Arctic, Vilhalmur Stefasson and George Wilkins photographed many aspects of Inuit culture, including the construction of this igloo.

Below: An Inuit craftsman uses a bow-powered hand drill.

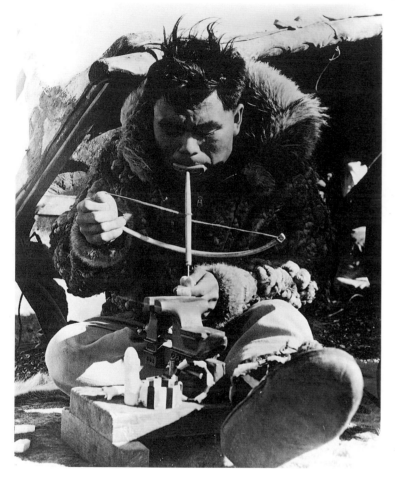

west are the Athapaskans (Athabaskans) of central Alaska and those parts of northern Canada west of Hudson Bay. To the south and east of Hudson Bay live the Algonquian-speaking peoples, who are related to those of the same linguistic group living around the Great Lakes.

Prior to the twentieth century, the lifestyle of the two peoples could not have been more different. For the Athapaskans, of whom the major tribes are the Chipewyans, Dogrib (Thlingchadinne) and Hare (Kawchodinneh), everything was geared toward mere subsistence, of which the key element was the caribou. Other game, such as moose and big horn sheep, were important, but the caribou was central to Athapaskan existence. It is theorized that these people followed the caribou migration across the Bering Land Bridge and first arrived in this region in 10,000 BC. Indeed, the Athapaskans' nomadic life continued well into the twentieth century.

Their nomadic lifestyle and their overwhelming need to address the matter of subsistence gave the Athapaskans little time to develop the elaborate religious life which evolved among tribes elsewhere on the continent. They did believe in the presence of demons and other specters from the spirit world, however, and shamans developed to deal with them.

In contrast, the Algonquians further south lived a virtually pastoral existence. These people, predominantly the various Cree tribes and the Ojibwa (Chippewa), lived in the expansive boreal forests north of the Great Lakes. They ate such delicacies as wild rice and maple sugar, fished the rivers that flowed through their territory and hunted the deer which populated the rich forests. In the summer, they camped in the sugar maple groves in the southern part of their range, tanning hides and building canoes. The Athapaskans also had canoes, but they were shorter than the bark canoes constructed by the Algonquians of the Subarctic and Northeast.

Notable places in the region where artifacts of the ancient native art and culture of the region may be viewed today include: the Glenbow Museum (Calgary, Alberta), the Carnegie Museum of Natural History (Pittsburgh, PA), the Alaska State Museum (Juneau), the Anchorage Museum of History and Art (Anchorage, AK), the Sitka National Historic Park (Sitka, AK), the Tongass Historical Museum (Ketchikan, AK) and the Prince of Wales Northern Heritage Centre at Yellowknife in Canada's Northwest Territories. At Pangnirtung in the Northwest Territories, the Augmarlik Interpretive Centre affords visitors the opportunity to meet and visit with the Inuit.

THE ORIGIN OF LIGHT
(An Inuit Legend)

Once there was a rich man who had a daughter. Outside his house stood a pole. It was dark, so he and his daughter put their fingers to their tongues and then to the wood to determine if the wood was green wood or dry wood. After all the people had brought water home from the well, the rich man's daughter went down to the well

to get water by herself. After she had gotten water, the raven and his helper, the squirrel, went to the well. The squirrel made a hole by the well and the raven became dirt and got inside the well. The next day, the rich man's daughter was again the last woman to get water. As she started to fill her bucket, the raven began thinking, 'I wish that woman would get thirsty and take a drink from her bucket!'

When she put her hands in her bucket to take a drink, she didn't realize she had dirt in her hands. She swallowed the dirt and tried to take it from her throat by coughing it up. When she got home, she told her father she had swallowed dirt. Then she became pregnant and had a baby boy with a tail.

The squirrel that had dug a hole by the well went to the rich man's house and made a hole under the front door. The woman's brothers–the boy's uncles–said, 'Our nephew has a little tail. He's got a little tail.'

When the boy started walking and talking, he told his mother that he wanted a big ball, but his mother told him that he might break it, so she gave him a small ball.

He kicked the ball and played with it. Watching him play, his uncles said over and over, 'Look at his tail! Look at his tail!'

When the boy was ready to go to bed that night, he gave the ball to his grandfather.

In the morning when he awoke, he asked his grandfather for his ball. After he played with it for awhile, he again begged his mother for a bigger ball. His mother told him, 'You might break that ball.' But his uncles gave him a bigger ball, which he immediately started to kick around the floor. Every time he kicked the big ball, he kicked it toward the front door. His

uncles gave him the smaller ball to play with, too, but the boy only wanted to play with the big ball. He kicked it toward the door, and out it went.

As soon as the ball rolled outside, the squirrel caught it with his teeth and started running away with it. The boy ran out the door after the squirrel, and his rich grandfather followed close behind.

When the grandfather got close to the squirrel, the squirrel threw the ball to the boy, and when the grandfather came close to his grandson, the boy threw the ball back to the squirrel.

Soon the grandfather became tired of running after them and stopped to rest, shouting, 'Dirty raven, dirty raven! Let your friends have half of it.'

The rich man explained to his grandson that if the raven had the smaller ball, the Inuit would have short days, but if the raven took the bigger ball, people would have long days.

However, now the Inuit have daylight because the raven took that ball and ran away with it.

THE ORIGIN OF FIRE (An Inuit Legend)

Once there was a man, his wife and their son, who lived down river from a village. They'd always heard that their was a man someplace with fire. The Inuit of the village always went to this man hoping to get fire, but they never came home again. The son wondered how they went to get fire, so he went to stay with his uncle in the village to try and find out where the man with the fire lived.

The boy asked many of the people where the man with the fire was, but nobody could tell him because the people who went to get fire never returned. Then the boy asked the older people in the village where the man with the fire was, but they didn't know either. Finally, the boy asked a very, very old man, who showed him the trail to the man with the fire.

When the boy found out about the trail, he left in search of fire. He traveled all autumn and all winter. He traveled into the summer and into the next fall and next winter. During a second summer, as he traveled, he got close to the place about which the very old man had told him. He came to a river and went down to the beach. According to what the old man had told him, the man with fire was across this river. He looked around and saw a line of big rocks far apart that stretched across the river.

'Maybe if I can take long steps, I can make it across,' he thought.

After he crossed the river, he walked up toward a steep hill. On the way he saw some old bows and arrows that had belonged to the men who had tried to get fire before. When he reached the top of the hill, he saw another hill far off in the distance, and in the valley below there was a house. He saw a man come out of the house, so he hid on the hill.

The man stood in front of the house and looked around, then went back inside. The boy thought to himself, 'I won't

get to that house if I stay a boy.' So he used the amulet hanging around his neck to become a squirrel.

As the squirrel got closer to the house, the man came out again and looked around. After he went back in, the squirrel stopped and thought to himself, 'I'm not going down to that house as a squirrel,' so he used his amulet again and became a piece of duck down.

Soon the wind came and blew the duck down and it landed in front of the house. The man in the house didn't come out, so he used his amulet once more and became a boy again. He waited outside for awhile. He didn't hear any sounds, and he crept up to the window and opened it. He looked down and saw a man sitting by the door with fire in his lap.

As the boy looked down through the window, he wondered to himself why his parents gave him the two little dolls he had inside his parka. He took them out and and, as he put them in the window, they began to dance.

The man with fire in his lap saw the two dolls and said, 'Go ahead, dance.'

The boy went to the door while the dolls were dancing and went inside. The man with the fire was still watching the dolls dance in the window. While the man was thus preoccupied, the boy took the fire from his lap and ran quickly out the door with it. He kept running to the steep hill and down the hill. When he got close to the rocks on which he had crossed the river, he looked back and saw the man running after him. The man shouted, 'I'll kill you if I catch you!'

The boy jumped the rocks across the river again. When he had gotten across, he looked back and saw that the man had stopped because he couldn't jump the rocks. The man called out to him. 'Since I can't get it back, you must share that fire with other people.'

After a journey of three years, the boy returned home. It was fall when he reached his uncle's village, and he went to his uncle's house to share the fire with him, and he went home to his parents. This was how the Inuit got fire.

Basket without a Lid
Thompson River Culture, early twentieth century
(imbricated surface)

Snow Goggles

Inuit, early twentieth century
(carved wood)

  These carved wooden goggles are used to help protect
the wearer against snow blindness.

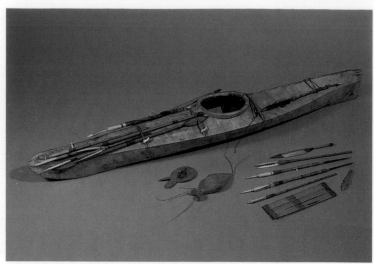

**Model of a Three-hatch Skin Boat
with Three Human Figures**
Aleut, late nineteenth century
(carved wood and leather)

Note the rain hats, particularly the one worn by the
man in the center.

Model of Kayak with Spears
Inuit, late nineteenth century
(carved wood)

Model of an Open Skin Boat with Rowers
Aleut, late nineteenth century
(carved wood)

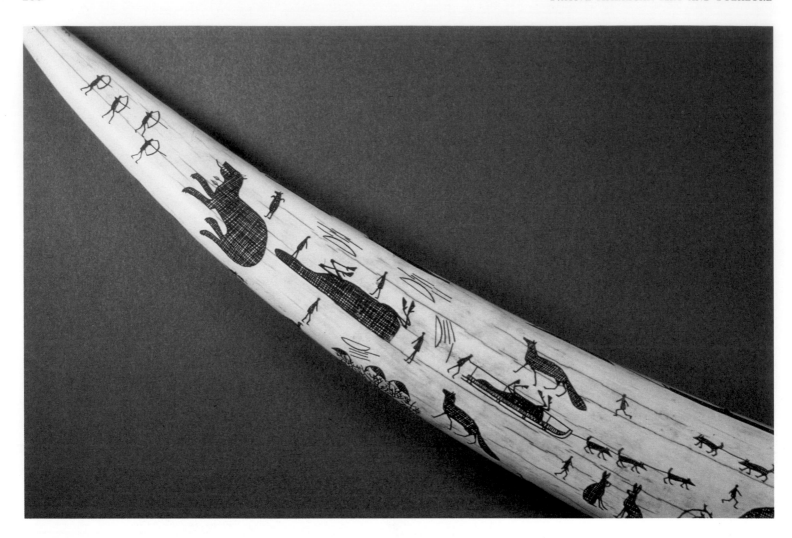

Hunting Scenes
Inuit, late nineteenth century
(carved walrus tusk)

The artifacts on these pages clearly show the evolution
of Inuit pictorial style as the carvers become aware of,
and begin to emulate, Western style.

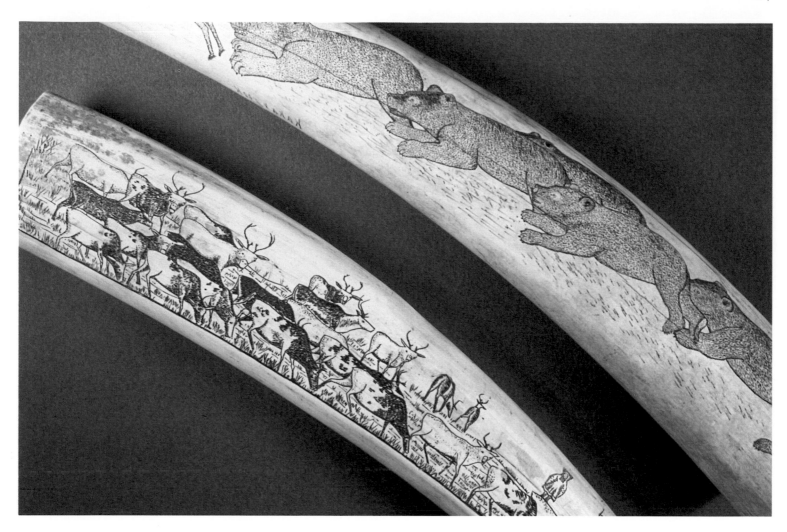

Bears and Caribou
Inuit, early twentieth century
(carved walrus tusk)

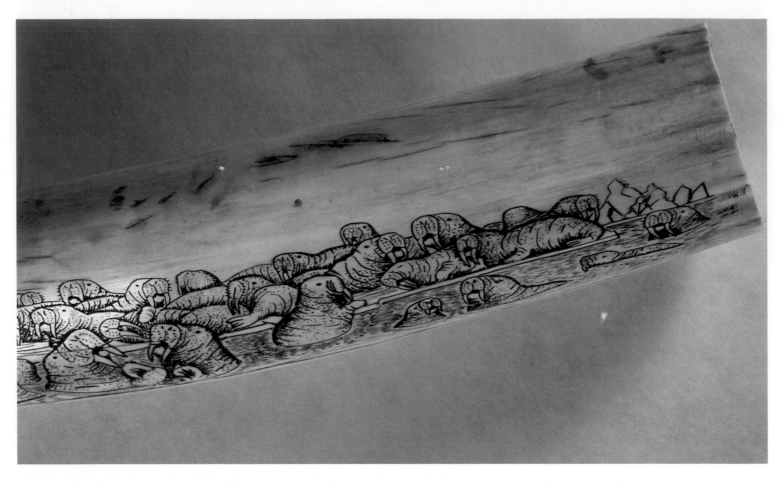

Walruses on Ice Flow
Inuit, early twentieth century
(carved walrus tusk)

   The influence of Western art, lacking in the piece on
the facing page, is obvious in this piece.

Hunting Scenes
Inuit, nineteenth century
(carved walrus tusk, 7.5″ high)

Hunting Spears
Inuit, nineteenth century
(wood, with ivory detailing)

The Inuit used a variety of weapons for hunting. The spear on the left was used in conjunction with an atlatl, or thrower, for catching fish and birds. An atlatl allows the hunter to maintain more distance between himself and his prey and increases the momentum of the spear. It is attached to the spear by a long tie of rawhide. The two harpoons to the right were used for hunting walruses. The removable head, which was attached to the spear by a long, flexible line, remained in the body of the animal. This spear was then used like a fishing pole to retrieve the prey.

Box in the Form of a Seal
Inuit, early twentieth century
(carved wood)

Leisler and Ivory Fishing Lure
Inuit, early twentieth century
(wood, ivory and bone)

The lure is dangled in the water to attract the fish, while the leisler (spear) is used to recover the fish. The central prong pierces the fish, and the two side prongs hold the fish in place to keep it from escaping. Fishing with a spear is most effective in shallow water or in weirs built to trap large numbers of fish. The prongs are carved out of musk ox antlers and the sharp prong out of bone. The lure has been decorated in a delicate pattern.

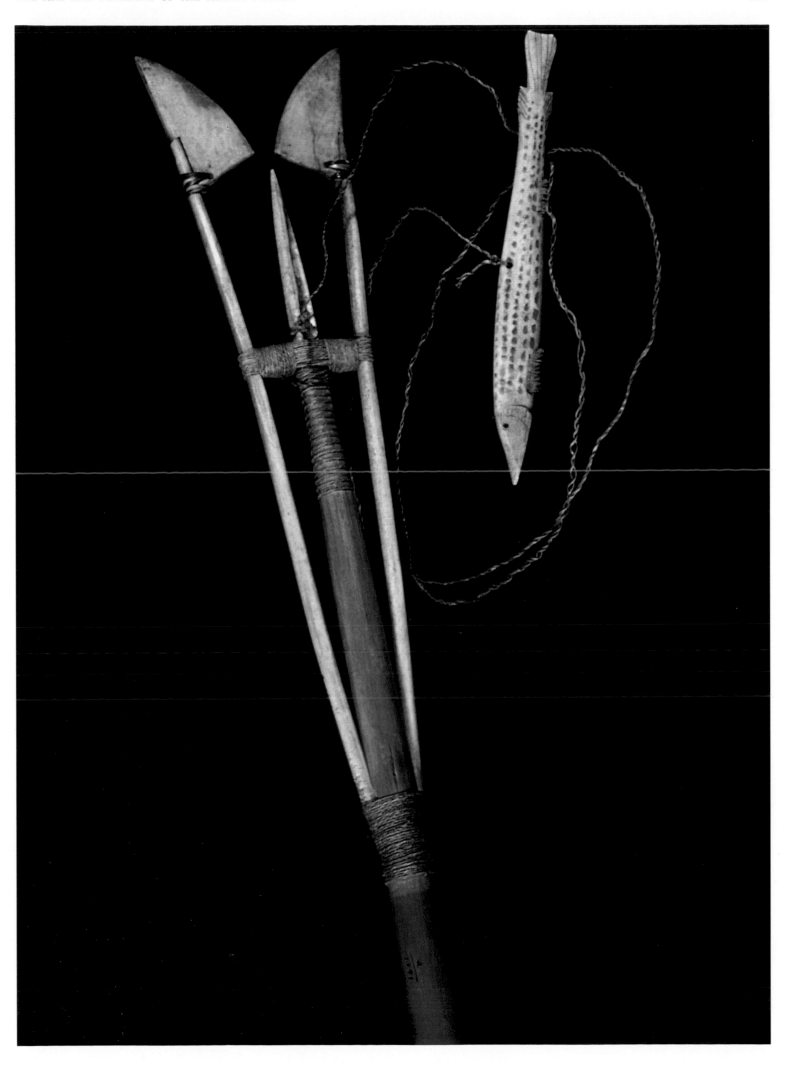

Crow Mask
Inuit, nineteenth century
(carved wood)

During long, Arctic winter nights, Inuit men carved
masks representing various spirits, who would be imper-
sonated in ceremonies. The masks were usually carved
from driftwood and designed under the direction of a
shaman. The shaman was the intermediary between the
physical world and the spiritual world, and a mask would
be inspired by his visions. At the same time, masks
representing animals were used for secular ceremonies.

An abundance of demons and deities inhabited the
Inuit world and were significant in their culture and daily
life. During ceremonies, men wore masks and danced
vigorously. Women wore small finger masks, often dupli-
cates of those worn by men, and danced behind the men
in a gentle, swaying fashion. For important ceremonial
dances, a large, square drum suspended from the ceiling
was played.

**Mask in the Image of a Being with Two Arms or
Flippers Seen Only by a Shaman**
Inuit, late nineteenth century
(carved wood)

Abstract Face Mask
Inuit, nineteenth century
(carved wood and leather thong)

This mask from the Lower Yukon River area is unusual
for its asymmetrical design. Masks were generally the
largest pieces of art that Inuits produced, and many were
painted in bright colors. Abstract masks, reserved for
religious ceremonies, were often very complex or ob-
scure in design, and their significance was understood
only by the shaman who directed the project.

Hunting Gear
Inuit, early twentieth century
(leather, ivory, and wood)

Adze Heads

Inuit, early twentieth century

(stone and ivory)

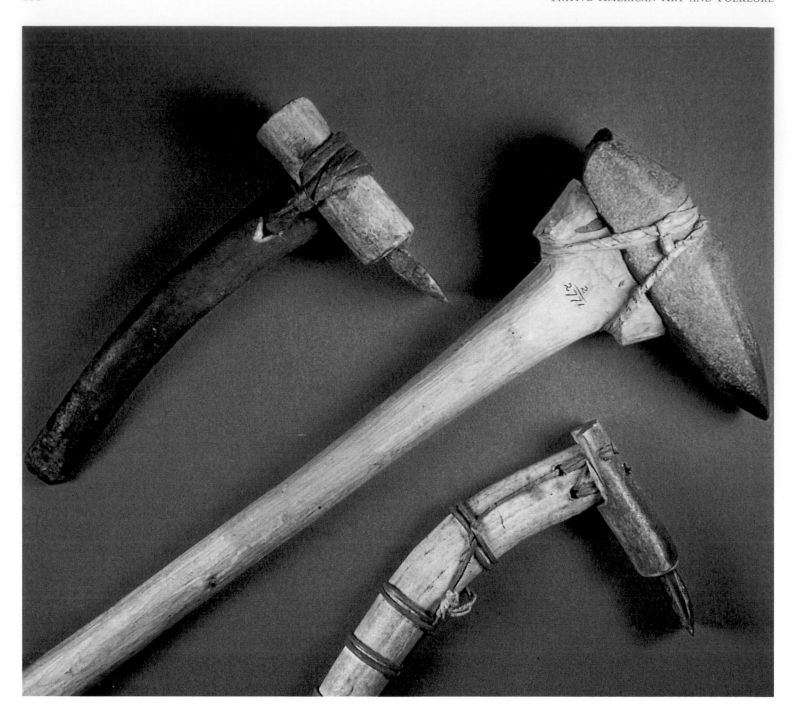

Three Adzes

Inuit, early twentieth century

(stone)

Two Dolls

Inuit, early twentieth century

(leather and wood)

(Please refer to *The Origin of Fire*, on page 201.)

Koryak Man (closed)

Denise Wallace (Aleut, Prince William Sound)
(sterling silver, 14k gold scrimshawed fossilized walrus
tusk, lace agate, silicated chrysacholla, 4″ × 1¾″)

'My jewelry is a way of saying, "This is who I am. This
is where I'm from,"' Denice Wallace says of her art. 'I
think of myself as a storyteller. My grandmother used to
tell me stories when I was young and I incorporate some
of them into my work.'

Koryak Man (opened)

Denise Wallace (Aleut, Prince William Sound)

Tlingit Man

Denise Wallace (Aleut, Prince William Sound)
(sterling silver, 14k gold scrimshawed fossilized walrus
tusk, 4″ × 1¾″)

Denise Wallace's jewelry are history lessons in themselves. With every piece she creates there's a story that
belongs to it—most of which hails from Alaskan folk-
lores of transformation.

Woman with Baby
Denise Wallace (Aleut, Prince William Sound)
(sterling silver, 14k gold, sugalite scrimshawed fossilized
walrus tusk, lace agate, 3¼″ × 1½″)

Kodiak Bird Mask
Denise Wallace (Aleut, Prince William Sound)
(sterling silver, 14k gold scrimshawed fossilized walrus
tusk, variscite, lapis lazuli, 3″ × 4″)

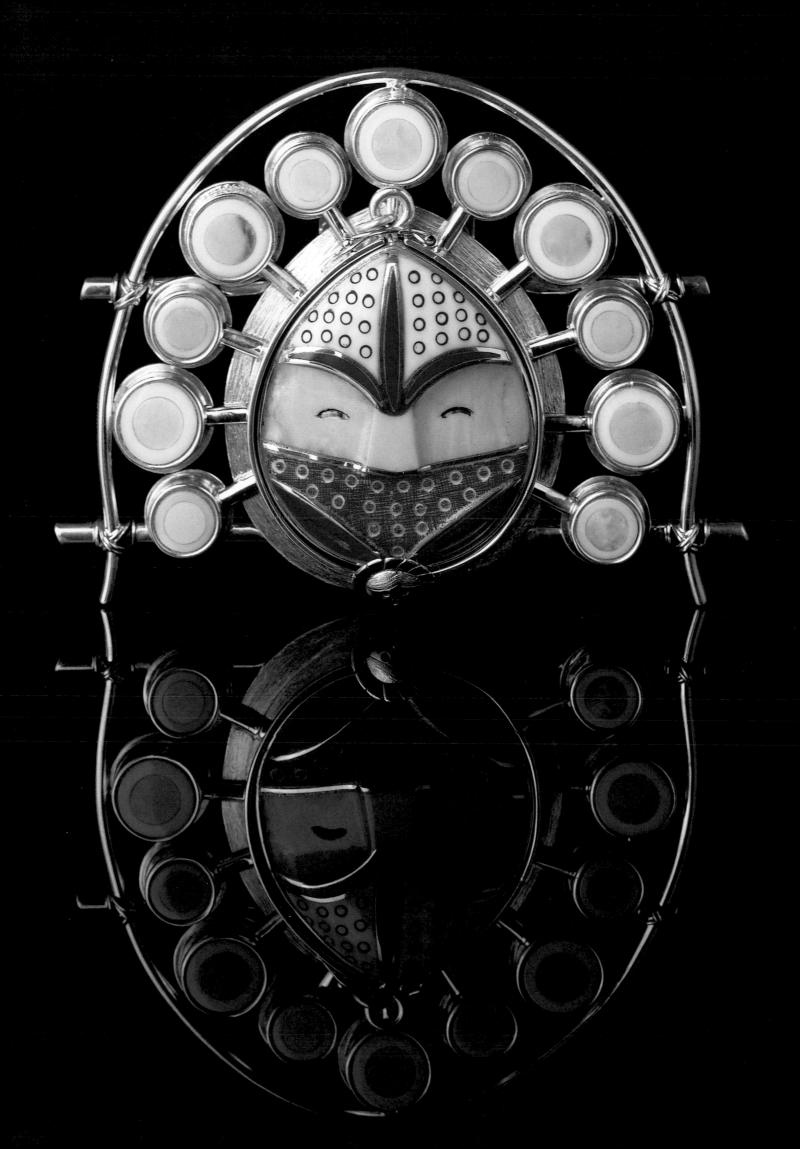

INDEX

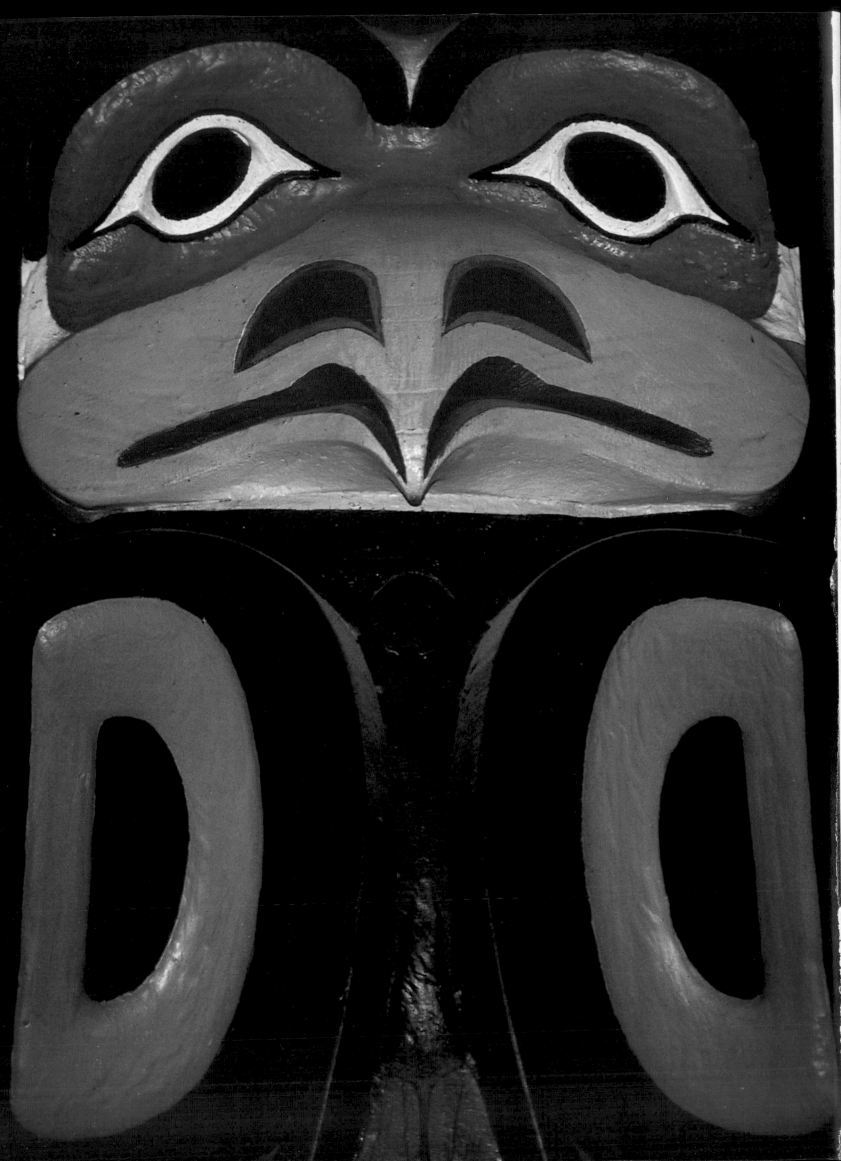